HELL HOUSE

A TALE OF TWO PSYCHES

SARAH MARTIN

For Andrea!
Sarah Martin
AKA Sheri Wilson
2022

SARAH WRITES

ISBN – 978-1-7782005-0-2

COVER DESIGN: Sarah Writes

first edition

CONTENTS

For every parent who has ever sacrificed for their child...
And for every adult child who never knew.

"You gain strength, courage, and confidence by every experience in which you really stop to look fear in the face.
You are able to say to yourself, 'I lived through this horror. I can take the next thing that comes along.'

You must do the thing you think you cannot do."

~ Eleanor Roosevelt

PROLOGUE

L ast year, 2016, was an undeniably wild ride, with circular arguments, trauma and blessings — and prolific, unforgettable lessons at every turn. For me, 2016 saw me compete in bodybuilding for the last time — at age 61, with the BC Provincial Championships. While I toyed with competing at Nationals for 2017, simply because I was qualified and it was an option available to me, the downturn that late-2016 brought to Matthew, and to me, ended the competitive fitness pursuits I had enjoyed since 1999. After two years of dieting and training, dropping 120 pounds to do a comeback to the stage in late 2015, and then Provincial Championships in 2016, well — let's just say it was probably time to hang the posing suit!

It's been tragic and disappointing to see how many people have come and gone from our lives, but equally a blessing to see who remains — who truly matters (and who seems to consider us important, too).

Winds of change are definitely afoot now. I needed liberty from a career that had proven invaluable over almost four decades (invaluable to Matthew's advocacy (before and after the TBI), to our financial stability, to his legal challenges, but proved to be less than optimal for my mental health).

Mattie continues to assert that he wants a level of independence for his future, so there's a need for me to be positioned closer to him to help encourage and redirect from the foreshadowed warning signs I've seen surfacing in him once again. I don't believe he can remain on solid ground without me being closer in proximity, and should he fail in Kamloops, it would never be in his best interests to return to the environments in the Lower Mainland. Been there, done that — suffered for it and learned the lessons.

We all have to determine to what depths we will venture for our freedom, and nearly 18 years of TBI have presented circumstances worthy of combat status. Now, we both want to strategize a new future (together and separately), going forward.

Funding authorities told me, at age 46 (interestingly, my best and happiest year of life) that I was "an aging parent" and should step away. Well, there's no denying that, at age 62, I am now *officially* an aging parent. I need to continue the relentless pursuit of this plan to freedom because Matthew assuredly is deserving of the sacrifice and effort. I believe he deserves the chance to choose more of his own decisions and to learn strategies for doing that safely. If the past 18 years of TBI have been "the rehearsal", surely, we are now prepared for the goal performance.

Sometimes, I think Matt's frequent tendencies to decompensation reflect just how much he struggles to live life as an adult, being babysat and controlled at every turn. Yet, he still needs daily redirection to be more age-appropriate in his behaviors — though accommodated no more decision-making than a 10-year-old child. At age 42, confined to this living since the age of 24, I feel he is losing faith to continue his hopes for, at least, a semi-independent living.

I will warn you that the accounts you will read are raw and often devoid of censorship, whether reminiscent of the dedicated relationship between a mother and son over 44 years — or of the brutal terror experienced and survived because of brain injury, exacerbated by mental health challenges, addictions, dissociation, homelessness and longstanding patterns of historical gang violence.

The Tale of Two Psyches series is a bit of a salute to "Murphy's Law" (which, in its essence, proclaims "What can go wrong, WILL go wrong") and a narrative about how far society's understanding and treatment of brain injury has advanced in 20 years, along with how far we still have to go. It is less of a guide than it is an adventure in awareness and never-ending re-education.

This is less of a "don't let this happen to you" kind of story than it is a "don't forget what happened to Mattie and his mom" kind of story. Sometimes, to be forewarned is to be prepared.

WINDS OF CHANGE

"When the winds of change blow, some people build walls and others build windmills." ~Chinese Proverb

A s we sit here listening to the high-velocity winds outside, Mattie and I are grateful we have no commitments until 11 AM this morning! The Lower Mainland often experiences rain and high gusts of wind. The map opposite will lend some reference to the areas we have lived— and where I have worked and Matthew has been incarcerated, hospitalized, lived in failed group homes, and wreaked havoc in gang activities years ago. I am happy to be leaving the locale, at last.

Bless his heart, he has done so much. He's had so much over-stimulation this past week and is utterly exhausted. It's 8 AM now, and he is still sleeping (despite having gone to bed at 7 PM last night)! He has not had this much activity since he played football as a running back for John Oliver Secondary School back in the day! Heck, this relocation prep probably has lasted as long as his John Oliver "football career." Sad to think in those terms, but life changes on a dime with Mattie — which means life changes on a dime for *mom*, as well.

I slept from 7 PM and find myself truly exhausted in every sense of the word. But the winds of change are upon us now; two more days here in the Lower Mainland to complete our "goodbyes," to get a couple of last walks through nature, and then to venture to the next chapter of my life — closer to my son again, in Kamloops — a green to desert-type topography in an area in central British Columbia, known as the Thompson Okanagan. Both of us have lived in Kamloops and in Kelowna. You will find another map of that vicinity in Chapter Five of *HELL HOUSE*. That is how and where I intend to finish my years — close to what is most important to me. No more dreams to chase, no more wondering what direction my life will take.

The goal is to just go with the flow, contribute as much as I can to those around me, and find my peace and balance at last — all the while enjoying my final days in closer proximity to my son. After all, I can do little from this location, a four-hour drive away, should the mask slip again (from him or from a caregiving facility).

REMEMBERING WHERE WE CAME FROM

S ome dates don't require calendar reminders. Some dates reside deep inside our minds, forgotten until the day arrives, and BAM, like an alarm, we find ourselves smack in the middle of wondering how we managed to let that broadside us.

NOVEMBER 16, 2016
Fifteen years ago today (around 10 PM tonight, in downtown Vancouver), I got the call that my son had just undergone brain surgery. That first photo, below, is not even the worst that I saw (that pic taken days after his surgery). Gang members beat him intending to murder him and he spent seven months hospitalized between coma and rehabilitation. I was told he would not survive; then I was told he would not live past 35, then I was told he would never have the ability to learn, then for more than a decade, I fought to keep him out of institutionalization.

And that second photo, of course, was taken ten days ago on his 38th birthday. It is fitting that I pick him up today for a few days of quality time together! I could not be more thrilled that he is now happy, stable, thriving, and continuing to improve! My reason, my WHY — my Mattie!

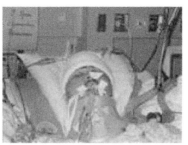

November 2001
Mattie on life support

Mattie, age 38
November 6, birthday suit!

Mattie reminded me to check the live camera footage for the Coquihalla Highway — British Columbia's own "Highway to Hell", as the popular television production affirms!

"Good reminder, buddy! See how you are improving?"

"I love you, Mom — you always make me feel good about myself. I truly appreciate that."

"Do you know what day it is today?"

"It's the day I get to spend with my beautiful mother!" he exclaimed.

"It's November 16th, buddy — 15 years ago today, you had your brain surgery."

"Wow — you remember that date? I don't remember it!"

"Oh buddy, I remember the important dates — every single one of 'em. And of course, it's a good thing you don't remember that day or the days leading up to that day, or months that followed that day."

"Mom, my last memory was watching those buildings fall on Nine-Eleven, and I can't even remember my first memories after my brain surgery. I don't remember being in that hospital. I think the first thing I remember was living at Ari's house. Wow! Mom, thank you for still being here with me, after everything I've put you through. I don't know why you love me so much, but I sure am glad you do. I am a lucky man."

It would appear, per the Coquihalla road cams, that the roadways are not looking bad right now and I am thankful for no snowfall overnight.

Coffee, a bath, and ten minutes of news, and we're off! I have my car loaded, and once we hit Timmy's for two coffees for the road, I begin my crawl of a drive to Kamloops (crawl, meaning there will be no 140kph stints along the way)!

In remembering Matthew's brain surgery, we can view it as a commemoration of progress — of just how VERY far he has evolved. We can regard today as another milestone toward the next steps in getting him to semi-independence. For all intents and purposes, it has become apparent that circumstances in the group home are declining now, with no indications of hope for a return to prior management protocols. I need to be in a more proximate location for an "on-call" response. Besides, it also presents an opportunity for positive change for myself, with a plan to part ways with a career that has (while supporting us financially through the years) caused my physical and mental health to decline.

Remembering where we came from can often transform the anxiety of an unknown future into a more acceptable perspective. Mattie suggested a "cheers" over how great life is now and how it is about to get much better! We touched our extra-large Tim Horton's cups together, said *L'chaim* in unison (and that warmed my heart since he has accepted and Anglican/Christian faith, rather than Judaism — it was his first adult, independent decision made after TBI. In Hebrew, *L'chaim* means "to life" — and Mattie certainly loved his), took a sip, returned them to the cup holder of the car, turned on some music, and I put the car in gear. We're off to Kamloops with the start of what will be a long and arduous move and an outstanding bonding opportunity!

WORK FOR WHAT YOU WANT

I t's November 17, 2016. We moved another load up to my Kamloops storage unit today. I'm becoming adept at navigating that Coquihalla Highway now, but I certainly would not say "I could do it blindfolded!" Blessed with good fortune, the roads have been acceptable, with only some minor slush in a couple of areas. My car is so filthy it looks like a bush pig, but all is well!

We will take another load up tomorrow. I will make a nice meatloaf stuffed with mozzarella cheese, some Bok Choy, mushrooms, and yams for the family I will work with. The plan is to drop that off, let them meet Mattie, then return to Surrey.

Matthew is here for another ten days! I am truly enjoying our time together, and the incredible bonding in the course of this "adventure." He calls it our "vacation." Poor guy, life has been so overwhelming, for as long as we both can remember, neither of us knows what a vacation feels like. I think the closest we have ever come to a "vacation" was the weekend at Harrison Hot Springs for his birthday last year. Yet, Mattie *never* complains.

Great day — utterly exhausted, but in a good way, not in the stress-from-a-crappy-office-experience kind of way!

In one of the beautiful moments shared with Mattie today, as we made our third trip by car to Kamloops to move another load of my belongings, it became even more apparent to me how consciously observant he is.

As we neared Hope, BC on the way back, he remarked about seeing my increased tension. I wasn't even aware of it. He told me, "Mom, my city is going to be so good for you; I noticed when we were there today that you relaxed. I loved to see you relax; now when we're getting closer to the Lower Mainland, you are tensing up again. You need to relax; I am so glad you are getting out of here. This is not good for you."

Wow... and then I again realized how important it was to live more "in the moment," cognizant of how fortunate I am to have my son and these next extended ten days with him!

NOVEMBER 18, 2016

We're now boycotting G Pizza Langley. I have loved the food from G Pizza (pizza, Indian food, wings) for a long time and I've ordered from every location out here, but the *Langley* location just messed up for the third time and I am done. Last night's order was delivered in *three* phone calls from them asking for directions (this is Surrey; we have easily identifiable addresses and logical numbers; my residential address is no exception). By the time the *especially rude* female staff snapped to ask our address again (being the same as what I provided to her twice before) and the driver phoned three times to ask how to get to us, our pizza arrived cold. Mattie insisted on handling the situation (I'm sure he was concerned about what might come out of my mouth; I do tend to be direct in these types of situations).

I was so proud of him as I stood outside, within earshot of him. First, the driver walked away with $4.75 owing in change; Matt asked for the money. The man said, "That's my tip." Matt told him, with no animosity in his voice, "Sir, the pizza is cold, so there is no tip." The man said he would not return the change, and Matt said, "Uncle, you *will* return the change. That is not your money." Matt stood there *oh so patiently* while the man pretended to search for the money, and ultimately produced every cent! Matt never lost his temper, never resorted to profanity or disrespect, and remained calm and respectful.

"Mom, I think I handled that one better than you would have."

I concurred — and feel incredibly proud of my young man, as just five years ago, he likely would have decked the man.

We measure progress one step at a time!

NOVEMBER 19, 2016

Holy crow, a whirlwind relocation maneuver to another city, over spectacular mountain ranges like this, is really a drain on the body and mind. I am so grateful to have Matthew's help. He has been invaluable both physically and emotionally and has been a G-D-send in watching over me (which has proven necessary in the last couple of days). After four trips to the Okanagan to put full carloads into storage, I am wiped out. I kept saying we had taken three loads, but *no*, it was, in actuality, four. Matt counted it out for me. Holy crow.

There is still much to complete before leaving, and only five working days to get it all accomplished, but I have a list/a strategy. We went to the mall earlier today and my PTSD was so triggered that I kept thinking I was at the Kelowna mall (no, that is not an error; we are moving me to Kamloops), and not in Langley. I kept saying, "This is so different; I do not know why I can't find my way around."

Matt was SO worried, as he sees the toll this has taken on me. I felt so disoriented; it was even more difficult for me to drive. Matt has had to follow behind me to make sure I turn the burner off the stove if I warm up any food. I am hoping for some downtime at home for a couple of days — and to only leave by vehicle when absolutely necessary.

This has to be truly hard on Mattie, too — but he has never once complained. He keeps telling me no matter what, no matter how much work this is, he is with me and that's where he would rather be than his group home right now. "Mom, my happy place is always with you, no matter what we are doing. I just want to be close to you. You are my life."

On many levels, I am in awe of him. I often take for granted that he is younger than me because of his deficits due to TBI.

In line with the change toward new beginnings and letting go of the past, I had to cull a few more so-called friends, many of whom only contact me when they want to ask for something, or to whine, bitch, and moan. None of them have once inquired about my health, knowing I continue to be on a waitlist for lung surgery. YES, there's a light at the end of the tunnel, and YES I have done everything possible and practical to turn a life around and into a different direction, but sometimes that means letting go of the "dead weight" from the past, as it will not serve me into the future. Rather, refusing to acknowledge the inevitable will only result in continuing frustration and disappointment. Life is far too abbreviated for this kind of nonsense and wasted time and effort.

There's always discomfort with any cleanse, but the end results remind us of why it is necessary.

What a whirlwind, driving seven to eight hours each day for three consecutive days. Poor Mattie woke up around 1 AM with a sore throat and sniffle, so I gave him two vitamin C and two vitamin D, along with a Hall's throat lozenge. We've done *so* much, pushing past our comfort zones with every drive, and I honestly don't know how well I would have fared without him there to help and keep me talking. That Coquihalla Highway, even with roads devoid of snow and ice is treacherous. We witnessed so many potential tragedies in the making. At one point, Mattie had remarked (seeing a van off the highway and turned onto its rooftop), "Bet those people never imagined their whole world would change today."

Yes, when our world is suddenly turned upside down, we seldom see it coming. I know this. I did not discuss the premise with Mattie, however. He perseverates on much inside that reprogrammed mind of his, and I'm trying to give him positive input to recall and focus.

On arising this morning, meeting in the kitchen for coffee around 5 AM, both of us remarked, "Wow! So glad we have a day off today!"

Well, we have a "day off" as in not making a round-trip to Kamloops, but there is still so much to accomplish. This mama has to go to Value Village and find a winter coat, as living in Kamloops will not be well-served Dec-April with the windbreaker

I've worn all winter for the past two years! Just yesterday, we had temperatures at minus three degrees (we are at seven above zero down here).

Then, my dear young man tells me this morning, "Mom, you're 62. I cannot believe how much you do. There is *nothing* lazy about you. I see how you push, and push, and push until you can't push anymore. I sure hope you learn to relax! But hey — know what Mom is upside-down? WOW! You are my Wow Mom and I love you! Thank you for wanting to be closer to me in my city."

Bless him, that's a recurring theme from my boy, but it is so wonderful to be loved that much, and to realize how observant and perceptive he is. He cannot remember what he did two hours ago most days, but he sure puts in concentrated focus where I am concerned. I am so lucky to know love like this and to be loved in return. It makes every TBI dance routine worth the effort.

I am utterly exhausted, but feeling so very blessed.

NOVEMBER 20, 2016

Whew; need a few hours today to recharge, and so does Mattie, bless his heart. He has not pushed himself this hard since before his brain injury; he's been so exhausted he just does what we now call "the nod." I can talk, a loud movie can be on — and it doesn't matter; unilaterally and without warning, his head drops and he's *out*. It's an unconsciousness that only lasts for a few seconds. It's odd yet morbidly fascinating to witness. Poor guy. He has helped me *so* much. Lazy was not a four-letter word in his vocabulary over these past days.

We are making another trip tomorrow to the storage unit. The car trunk is now full, and the back seat will accommodate a few more items as we venture out in the morning. We need to return to Kamloops to pick up more meds for Mattie as we've extended his time down here with me. Last night, he *begged* me not to make him go back to the group home yet. "Mom, can we just get my medication, say a friendly hello, smile, and hit the road again?" While that is endearing, it is disconcerting that he would rather work himself into an exhaustion stupor to be with me than to return to the group home. A year ago, that home was the best thing (besides me, in his words) that had happened in his life. Until recently, it always thrilled him to spend time with me, but he was equally excited to return to his home when our visit concluded. "Mom, that place is not the same now. It's just a place to eat and sleep. I try to avoid trouble by staying in my room as much as I can, but you know me — that's hard 'cause I'm a social butterfly!"

I am hoping the rain holds off long enough for us to take a walk. I truly need that exercise in my regimen again consistently; today marks Day One of full-on clean eating again, too. My blood pressure has been stupidly high lately and I need to smarten up with that since I live with a heart & stroke condition just under the surface. 155/90 and 157/92 are not good measurements, and I would not want to see that worsen. Time to return to a regimen of celery and asparagus with every meal again, four liters of water per day, vitamins are taken consistently, and exercise by any means necessary, every single day, even if it's "only" some stretching and arm circles at home.

As we sit here listening to the high-velocity winds outside, we're grateful we have no commitments until 11 AM this morning!

We have a day of relaxation ahead, saying goodbyes to our friend Shannon, and tomorrow we will spend some quality time with our beloved, longest-friend-ever, Desi.

Winds of change are upon us now! Let's get to building windmills!

NOVEMBER 24, 2016

I've been doing some advanced planning for my new job as a caregiver and homemaker. I've charted out some of the sample meal plans I will create for client Roxanne! The idea is to keep it as healthy as possible, but let her fully enjoy her final years. After all, she deserves that! She is soon to be 92! I don't eat pork or shellfish, but she apparently loves it, so she can bloody well have it! I'll keep it healthy as possible! All meal plans have been approved by her 72-year-old retired registered nurse daughter, Dolores   who lives in a home on the same property where my client's mobile home is about a 30-minute drive outside the city limits of Kamloops.

SAMPLE MEAL PLANS
Dinners, with leftovers as lunches through the week(s)
- CABBAGE ROLLS, with broccoli and yams
- BEEF OR CHICKEN STROGANOFF, with salad & roasted potatoes
- STUFFED PORK CHOPS (apples, bacon & feta), with red potatoes & green beans
- ROAST BEEF, with mashed potatoes & gravy, carrots & salad
- COCONUT CURRY CHICKEN, with spinach, oven-browned potatoes & sautéed mushrooms
- HAM with rutabaga, salad & sautéed green beans & onions
- Spaghetti & meatballs, with salad & garlic bread (homemade bread)
- Lasagne or ravioli with parsley/tomato salad & biscuits
- Roasted turkey legs with cauliflower & Brussel sprouts in cheese sauce
- Steak, with baked potato & sour crème & salad
- Beans with cornbread, asparagus, and creme-cheese mashed potatoes

DESSERTS
- Homemade puddings
- Carrot cake with lemon crème cheese frosting
- Chocolate cake with a frosting of choice
- Spice cake with white frosting
- Angel food cake with strawberries & whipped crème
- Banana pudding
- Pecan pie
- Apple pie

- Muffins
- Cookies (oatmeal/raisin, chocolate chip/cranberry, shortbread, coconut)

NOVEMBER 25, 2016

Fascinating, as I wind down for the final load to Kamloops, with my new direction, new employment focus, and living closer to my beloved son, I now see multiple emails arriving in response to job applications from two weeks ago. Offers have come in (four to be exact), and I am proud to graciously decline. I had posted my CV online with one website in Kamloops, and even received a job offer from a Vancouver law firm through *that* venue!

I am still feeling like I am in a dream, hardly believing this has transpired so quickly, with absolutely everything falling into place, step by step. I am finally at peace with so many issues that have plagued me for years, issues I have just worked around until now. Alas, there is zero doubt in my mind that I have made the right decision, and I am excited to move forward in this entirely new direction!

We watched another GREAT movie on Netflix: "Eddie the Eagle!" Absolutely outstanding, edge-of-your-seat excitement, and the true story of Britain's Eddie Edwards, a uniquely brilliant ski-jumper who stunned the world at the Calgary 1988 Olympics!

Mattie didn't like it or want to watch it in the first five minutes, but as any good mom would do, I forced it upon him! He LOVED it and told me, "Mom, you know me better than I know myself! Thank you for teaching me so much. Thank you for *seeing* me."

Thompson-Okanagan

Prince George

Alberta Rockies

McBride

Robson Valley

Mount Robso

Cariboo

Jas

Wells Gray PP

North Thompson

Williams Lake

Kootenz

Clearwater

Shuswap

Sun Peaks

Salmon A

Kamloops

Silver St

South Thompson-
Fraser
Canyon

Vernon

Okanagan

Lytton

Kelowna

Whistler

Big W

Lower
Mainland

Simil.

Penticton

Princeton

Vancouver

Osoyoos

50 km

Manning PP   Cathedral PP

NEW BEGINNINGS

I t's November 29, 2016 — and Day One with the new job. Roxanne, my 92-year-old client, is still sleeping.

Roxanne has a little raggedy poodle named "Sophie." I've fed Sophie, let her out and back in, got coffee ready, got the porridge ready to cook, and I have oatmeal muffins (with cherry, apple, cinnamon & raisins) in the oven! Sophie is around 20 years old. When I arrived here, Roxanne's daughter "sprung that one on me."

"Oh, I didn't mention there's a dog here. Hope that's not a deal-breaker." How does one respond to that? I think she was pretty confident I would not move my belongings back to the Lower Mainland and leave Kamloops at this stage! Besides, how much trouble could a raggedy, ungroomed little dog be? I've always loved dogs and cats (and horses), anyway. All good! I'm here to help!

Dinner tonight will be quiche and oven-roasted potatoes with salad! It is nice to have daily fresh eggs; these folks have 60 chickens (down from about 100, they say)!

DECEMBER 1, 2016

The group home has approved a request to pick up Mattie on Monday morning around 9 AM, that being a day off for me to celebrate my birthday.

Yesterday almost felt like a Spring day — sunshine, cool but very nice (no jacket required for me), until around 4 PM, then the temperature started dropping. I was up at 5:30 this morning, and BAM — we have snow.

Poor little Sophie came back all wet and semi-frozen! Her hair is long and very matted and, now, frozen. When a proper time presents, I will mention taking

Sophie to a professional groomer; perhaps that is something I could do for them on one of the days I have visitation with Mattie.

Guess it's time to stoke up the wood-burning stove! Yep, I'm becoming a country girl *fast*!

AND IT BEGINS!

COUNTRY ADVENTURES

I t has been truly wonderful being able to see my young man every week. The only thing that can prevent that is heavy snowfall. My little Chevy Sonic does not navigate snow well. All-season tires are insufficient for Kamloops winter weather conditions (and I cannot afford to purchase winter tires, or chains, at the moment). The area where I live is outside the city limits — near Kamloops Lake. Temperatures are easily and typically lower by about minus five to minus ten degrees in the countryside.

Matthew is so much more alert nowadays... His email to me just now:

> "I SENT GRAMMA AN E-MAIL SHORT AND SWEET!!
> IS IT SNOWING THERE HOPEFULLY URL BE ABLE TO
> MAKE IT HERE!! "

Cute, he always types in all caps! He's always shouting! And sweet that he is calling Roxanne "Gramma". Certainly, he knows it would be inappropriate to call her by her first name, and he cannot remember surnames. But, he can remember "Gramma"! She seems to enjoy that. She is fond of Mattie.

DECEMBER 3, 2016
Whew. Busy "day off!" Outstanding time with Mattie by my side moving two loads out of my storage unit and into my home (goal is to not pay another $101 per month for that unit... paid until Jan 10, so I have time to get it all back out of there

with Mattie's help!)... Dolores had suggested there was space for my boxes in the entry hallway — and assured me there was no issue with that. Nice!

After returning Mattie to the group home, I came back and finished two writing projects — one for a friend, and another one for pay.

I am thrilled to be pursuing an *entirely* different line of life satisfaction now. Although I can't buy a new pair of shoes just yet, it is nice to see my "stress-brain" on pause, at last!

DECEMBER 4, 2016

Country living — country *learning*! I couldn't get that wood stove going for the life of me yesterday morning... I think the two women here just assumed *anyone* knows how to start a fire in a wood-burning stove! They watched from the kitchen as I struggled with it, and never gave up. I then remembered camping years ago, and how I became the "kindling queen" and put on my coat, went outside, and looked for sticks. Fancy the difference dry kindling makes! Talk about a learning curve for this "city girl!" Both Dolores and her mother, Roxanne, watched in sheer entertainment!

Piece of cake this morning, easy as pie, however (food markers even for making a fire? Good grief!)! Roxanne will be pleased with the warm fire glowing when she wakes up! It's cold out here, currently at minus 10 degrees!

DECEMBER 5, 2016

WONDERFUL birthday with Mattie today! Went for a walk on the property... saw a herd of wild bighorn sheep and walked within 40 feet of them after following their tracks in the snow! An eagle flew overhead within about 15-20 feet of us, too! Matt was just thrilled!

Also visited the neighbors' llama herd. Matt was mesmerized until one animal spat on him! I have experienced this in the past, myself, so I could tell him that llamas rarely spat at people, but they *do* spit on each other frequently. It's their way of expressing irritation or annoyance with other llamas. Llamas that spit on humans were likely raised by humans, with little time around other llamas.

At the top of the hill, we had a gorgeous view of Kamloops Lake... so close! I forgot to take my cell phone, so we didn't get any pics... but next time, we will remember the phone!

Kamloops Lake
December 2016

We have been steadily moving small loads from my storage unit to my work location — a double-wide, three-bedroom trailer on a remote property. Given my remuneration is nominal, this will save me about $100/month. I hope to have the unit vacated by Saturday; there should be a refund applicable since I paid an extra month in advance. Mattie, bless him, told me to never do that again. "Mom, I know you always want to do the right thing, and you're always worried about stuff going wrong... but this time, you could be out a hundred bucks — and that's a lot of Timmy's coffee!"

Things continue to be awry with the group home. I am hopeful it is merely "growing pains" and a transitional phase for new management. I try to like her, but I do not — and I can't decide whether I am so biased with having adored and respected Angela before, or whether there is a personality deficit there. My "Spidey Senses" explode when I detect any reminders of what I have observed with very negligent "caregivers" in the past.

I had to email management when he visited me with no cigarettes. I purchase his cigarettes each month, so I know he has a supply there. "In the future, when Matt comes to visit me, could he please bring cigarettes with him? This morning, he tells me he asked the staff for cigarettes to take with him for the day (to last until around 3 PM) and they denied him. Staff only gave him one cigarette first thing in the morning. I will not be purchasing cigarettes for his day visits with me now, so he will need to bring smokes. Hoping that is not a problem!"

Experience has taught me far too well to avoid any behavioral triggers caused by a short supply or *no supply* of cigarettes. After all, it was the denial of a cigarette years ago that found me assaulted and injured — and Matthew in Forensics for 18 months. That was 18 months of life neither of us could ever take back.

WHEN THE HONEYMOON FADES

I have been on the job for almost a month now. It's December 12, 2016, and I am utterly trapped. Yes, you read that right.

I finally had a decent night's sleep last night, but I took two Valium to achieve it. I've been up since 5:30 AM, however, I feel rested. My back is still sore from lifting Roxanne in the bed, the night before last. She has full use of her legs, can transfer from wheelchair to commode, wheelchair to bed, and she apparently can transfer and push herself over to the center of her bed.

I was told at the time of hiring, specifically, that there would be no heavy lifting. The occasional need to deter to something that works for the circumstance will occur from time to time, I presume. Hopefully, this will be nominal.

I miss my exercise routine, going to the gym... but I cannot leave the house for *any purpose* for five days. I am on-call 24-7 here for those five days. Again, I feel a little trapped and imprisoned.

I also resent having to be up from 6 AM to 10 PM. I feel I have lost my freedom, and for what? To only have a roof over my head, and food in the fridge (which I do not even get to choose for myself)? Yes, I came here and took this position to be closer to my son — but it's already apparent that this scenario has the potential for disaster. Not only is the nutrition provided here something other than I would choose for myself — with all red meat here, pork, shellfish, chicken thighs, and insufficient green vegetables for my needs), but more disconcerting than that, I detect escalating personality changes with both Roxanne and her daughter. Something is not right here. Perhaps there is more than meets the eye in this environment.

I find myself "stress eating" now and have gotten into a terrible habit of eating ice cream late at night. I find myself enraged with Roxanne's increasing demands and the whining of the dog. The dog is 22 years old, not 20, and I think she is unhealthy. I frequently have to clean up her vomit throughout the trailer, and she often refuses to eat. I suggested she might need to see a veterinarian, and that she needs professional grooming. A badly matted dog suffers health complications because of it, but Roxanne snarled, "Mind your own business. She's old — and she is just fine."

Okay, but wow. That left me a little stunned. I guess the honeymoon phase has concluded already. It's abundantly clear that she enjoys having power over those around her — perhaps because she feels she has no power of decision-making with daughter Dolores making all her decisions for her. Roxanne is also trapped as an elderly and incapacitated senior. What a mess — she's trapped, I'm trapped — and Mattie is feeling trapped (in a declining group home, and with brain injury deficits for life).

Yesterday, I was tired of seeing the filthy fridge. G–D only knows how long it's been since it saw a proper cleaning. I could not stand idly by and look at the residue and filth under the seams below the glass shelving. It took me three non-stop hours of comprehensive cleaning, but it's now pristine.

There was no gratitude for having done something that was not within my expected duties. I think they don't even notice it is dirty. I mentioned to Roxane's daughter, Dolores, that I'd cleaned it and how long it took (feeling proud of my hard work), and her response was "Well, EXCUSE me!"

I am seeing more and more "WTF" moments in this household. WTF serves a couple of applications, for me, including "Where's the funding?" But let's redirect this line of negative thinking!

POSITIVES

I do love being in Kamloops and believe the locale will be good for me. If I compare things with the Lower Mainland, here I see calmer, friendlier people... and, of course, I am a brief 30-minute drive away from Mattie. This is what I need, so I surmise a little more suffering for a few months can be justified since I achieved a timely goal in getting myself positioned near my son.

PLANS

Once I can file my income tax return, I should see about $3,000 coming my way with that refund. Those funds will finance my "escape" from this place I already call Hell House (inside my mind; I never want to express that verbally, and I never want Matthew to know my opinion of the place). I have calculated a plan...

I will need to ensure I have money for rent, a half-month deposit, a bed, and other preliminary basics.

It will be inevitable that I will need to give up the vehicle... I need to be taking the bus now since I cannot afford a car, insurance, fuel, and vehicle maintenance. I can no longer afford the luxury of a vehicle if I am not pursuing a career in law.

I am trying to imagine brighter days, in my personalized décor, with my personal kitchen items, with groceries of *my choosing*, and the ability to train in a gym again... These are the dreams that keep me going; otherwise, I feel as though I am entrapped, living this ugly little life in this ugly little trailer with this ugly furniture and this annoying whining dog, trapped and unable to leave... all to pay for a car I cannot afford, which sits in the driveway five days a week.

When the honeymoon fades, the issues come out of the woodwork.

TAKING THE BAIT

Dolores phoned around 8 PM, apparently to say she did not feel like coming down to her mother's trailer. When Roxanne answered her phone, I was in the kitchen behind her, washing dishes. I heard her say, "She's in her room." WTF? Did she forget already I just walked past her, and I was in the kitchen? Or is she playing Devil's Advocate and making trouble? I've observed that she enjoys that.

When I came into the dining area, she said sheepishly, "Dolores just phoned. I phoned her back to see if she needed anything. She said no, she was just checking to make sure everything was okay."

9 PM: Thankfully, it is almost time to turn off the lights for Roxanne. I am truly irritated with her right now. I spent three hours today making her an alphabetized Address/Telephone Directory, consolidating and organizing alphabetically three of her jumbled telephone books, and random scraps of papers with scribbled notes. To correct those she had written incorrectly, I looked up postal codes. She did not even *glance* at it — and she never said thank you. It was a significant amount of work, but it was also an opportunity for me to learn.

Lesson learned? DO NO EXTRA — it is not appreciated, and it will even be judged as a criticism of what is already here. Improvements are considered judgment of what was not working. WOW.

THEN, she asked me what her iPad charge level was registering; I plugged in the charger. "Does that say 13 percent?" I did not have my reading glasses with me, and she knows well that my vision is significantly impaired. I reminded her I could not read it. She could completely read it and promptly read it to me. "It says 13 percent — right here." She added, "You really have to see an optometrist and get your eyes checked." She had set me up for that, and I took the bait!

I told her AGAIN (this is about 10x since I've worked here), that I cannot see an optometrist or get prescription lenses. There is no money for that.

Retorting in what has become her typical disparaging tone, "Money or no money — you need to get 'em checked."

"Roxanne, I don't think you understand: there IS NO MONEY for that nor will there be in the foreseeable future; I can't get blood from a stone." I stood up, walked into the kitchen, and pretended to be washing dishes again. I only answered questions posed to me for the balance of the evening and I put her to bed at 8:45. I set my alarm for 9:30 PM, her official "lights out" timing, per Dolores' instructions.

Decision made. I will be seeking alternate employment shortly after the Christmas holidays. I will be discreet, and I might be stuck here until March, but in any event, I feel bad about leaving Dolores stranded, so I will hang in here as best I can — for Dolores (not for Roxanne). Roxanne is old. I know she is mostly miserable. And I completely see why caregivers have not stayed. I will not be staying either.

Since Roxanne was still reading, I let her continue until 9:45. When I finally went in and *tried* to be nice, saying, "Ready to sleep?" Her response was a resounding, "NO! I'm wide awake." I said nothing, just stood there rather dumbfounded. She took off her glasses, declaring defeat (and likely not wanting to suffer the wrath of Dolores learning she refused to go to sleep at her usual time), and asked me to pull all the blankets up around her shoulders, which I did.

I gave her a "sweet dreams" in my most pleasant and softer voice.

Then, as I walked away, turning out her lights, she commanded again, "Turn the light out in the bathroom."

"Roxanne, there is no light on in the bathroom."

"Look at it," she growled, "There is!"

I don't get it — why the commanding, disrespectful tone of voice? I told her, "No, that is the light in my bedroom. As I walk back down the hall to my room, I need it to guide me." I am absolutely livid, but I keep that to myself where it belongs.

Then, with all this nonsensical banter, Sophie was still outside, and I never heard her bark and had not let her back in. Dolores, or her husband Dave, must have heard her and let her in because she was walking around the trailer and looking at me, lost and confused. I let her into her crate and gave her two dog-treat rewards. She is conditioned to exit for a final pee-and-poop at night, and trots back inside the open door of her crate, patiently awaiting a dog treat before the door to the crate is closed.

I will need to apologize to Dolores in the morning for not hearing Sophie bark; otherwise, there will be hell to pay with Dolores *and* with Roxanne.

BULLYING IS BULLYING, NO MATTER THE PAY

W e're not even halfway through December, today being December 12, 2016, and I am strategizing an exit plan for March.

I've planned with the group home to pick up Mattie on Thursday morning and return him on Friday around 3 PM (I have two

consecutive days off, thankfully, and he will spend the night out here with me). There are two twin beds in my room.

And Roxanne's melodrama continues. After seeing me perform my morning floor exercises (15 minutes' worth), she snarls, "You need to stop worrying about your weight; just walk up the hill and back, that's all the exercise you need. Why did you only have soup for lunch? Why didn't you have a hamburger too? Cheese won't make you fat. You are being ridiculous."

Where is all this coming from? As I listened to her drone on, with what seemed to be an illogical rant, meant to distress and distract me, her other comments included: "GMOs in corn just mean the kernels are bigger."

"Organic doesn't make any difference; there are chemicals everywhere."

"Why do you worry about taking a sleeping pill? Why would you want to wean off those? Just take the bloody pill and get your sleep. You look tired."

"Your haircut is crooked. I hope you didn't pay for that. And you need those bangs out of your eyes." This critique was uttered in reference to my $50 asymmetrical cut.

"Why don't you have any money? What are you wasting all your money on" (after which I explained that the $800/month she pays me, with my car payment, gas, insurance, MSP, and cell phone bill, leaves me with a residual of about $4 per month)? Yeah — I have money: $20, twice a month!

DECEMBER 13, 2016
I tried to sleep without a pill last night (as I only have two left) but awakened around 1 AM and had to take one.

Now, at 5 AM, I tip-toe to the bathroom to not wake up Sophie the dog. I cannot go to the kitchen to make coffee without waking her up, and I am not in the mood for that incessant whining to start.

Today is the day Cody, the care aide, comes in for Roxanne's bath. I have four hours to call my own (since bathing Roxanne is not part of my assigned duties), so I will work on my taxes. I might drive into the city to top up the gas tank at Canadian Tire, but otherwise, I have only $20 to my name and cannot be wasting gas needlessly. I used some time yesterday to prepare Roxanne's organized contacts (with no thanks and

without her even viewing it), and did not begin my income tax preparation as planned. Today, no more freebies; I attend to my own priorities after my work is completed. I need that tax refund at the earliest viable opportunity.

This morning, I will vacuum, mop floors, and dust. Then, the house is clean. I do not care for the care aide Cody, and feel she is surly and entitled. I also don't like the work ethic she has shown thus far. Since she did not do *her* job well last time, with no liner in the commode pot, dirty dishes left in the sink, no laundry done, and she left the back porch door to the laundry room open... I don't want her criticizing *my* duties, so I am a bit more attentive to early completion than usual.

6 AM now. It's time to get the wood fire started and make coffee. Here comes the whining dog syndrome for another day. It is what it is. This is my life, for now!

Cody arrived late (20 minutes), and gave no call to say she was running late, and no apology on arrival. I don't like her, but I don't have to engage with her. Our duties do not "overlap." Now 10:28, I heard Roxanne ask for her bath — and Cody had the intestinal fortitude to say, "Maybe after I get more water in? I have to drink a lot of water." WTF? She is not a volunteer; she is paid well by the health authority for her services.

I found it fascinating that Roxanne offered no snarls or judgment to Cody!

Roxanne started in on money matters again with me this morning. "WHY does it cost you $700 to run your car every month? That should be under warranty." I explained the inevitable, unchangeable expense to her AGAIN (fuel, car payment, insurance, maintenance)... Then she told me I should get an engine block heater for the car. I told her there was no money for that. She said, "Well, I would always want to know how much it was, so I could save for it."

And, of course, a further circular debate ensued. I explained AGAIN (and I'm getting sick of doing that — I am not 16 years old) that I have $20 left, twice a month. There's no money to be saved. That goes for coffees for Matt and *maybe* my Synthroid medication every 90 days. There is no money left for sleeping medication either... and certainly no savings in the mix.

I explained to her that in the future when she transfers to Gemstone, a senior's care residence for which she is on a waitlist, I would sell my car. She said, "Well, then you won't get to see your son." She was assuming I would stay on once she left the property for a senior's residence — and simply live here, care for her dog, and pay rent to Dolores! Not a snowball's chance in hell on that one.

"Oh yes, I will see my son. I will move to the North Shore, in the city, and take a bus — and he can learn to take the bus to see me."

"OH," she said, "There's a bus route there?"

I told her yes, that buses operate throughout the city — for visiting, for getting to the doctor, for grocery shopping. She said nothing further. I think she also hopes I would stay on board here when the trailer is empty, supervise the property, pay rent and take care of the dog.

Cody arrived late again today, once again with no call to say she would be late (AND she left on time). All she did was complain about how hot it was, how the wood stove was too hot and should be turned off — criticizing *me*, asking why I put two beanbags in the kitchen. WTF.

Each night when Roxanne prepares for sleep, I heat two beanbags in the microwave, and place those at the foot of her bed, under the covers. She is thin and frail and seems to always be cold. This is all done per Dolores' protocols and instructions. I merely follow directions.

Cody then asked Roxanne in a negative tone, "Is it her day off?"

I despise this woman. She did not change the commode bag, despite Roxanne telling her to do so. She told Roxanne, "I'll do that *next* time — no

need to do it twice since you'll be going again." And Roxanne said nothing. WTF.

Turns out, I have another opportunity to learn. It's not just law firms where women bully and negatively compete for attention!

Cody did the laundry (part of her designated duties) but failed to fold anything properly — not done in the manner in which she finds things in the drawers. She also did not close the door between the laundry room and the mudroom on her way out (AGAIN, she did the same thing last week, and I was scolded by Dolores for leaving it open). Cody has no attention to detail and no pride in a job well done.

I ALMOST told Cody, when she was leaving, next time she wants to criticize anything I do here, say it to my face... but I opted to wait on that until the time that I give notice. She had an undeniable attitude when saying a curt goodbye to me, and I returned the tone. I refuse to pretend I like her. I don't get paid enough to bullshit like a politician or a lawyer, and I am already approaching my *wit's end* with this nonsense.

But the annoyance continues, despite my trying to remain perky, positive, and minding my own business. I did push-ups again. Two days ago, I could only perform five; today, I could execute eight, with good form.

Roxanne again expressed her criticism, "I really don't know about you. All that is unnecessary."

I am *hating* it here now. It's going to be a *long* wait until March.

8 PM and my irritation spreads like crabgrass. I keep *trying* to bring things around to positive laughter and smiles — but Roxanne just keeps asking for more. Tonight, she asked me to trim the dog's toenails, because the groomer didn't do it. I politely refused, saying that was outside my comfort zone.

"Sophie has a groomer? It's been while, eh? She is in dire need of having that matting shaved down. I could drop her at the groomer in the City one day and bring her back on a day off?"

She insisted, "I have clippers." I refused. She gave me a dirty look. "You've clearly never had a dog — you don't shave a dog in the winter, stupid."

"Well, winter only started a month ago — and the length of her fur says she's not been groomed for more than a year, I'm guessing. That could be the foundation for her whining and deteriorating health."

"Well, you can cut her toenails — the clippers are over there in that drawer." She turned in her wheelchair and pointed to a drawer in a china cabinet, six feet away.

I am *not* hired to groom the dog, and I *will not* do it.

"Would you like some more tea?" I asked, changing the subject.

Then, because Cody the idiot care aide did not wash the tea out of Roxanne's knitted doily, which she uses to keep her iPad stabilized, Roxanne asked *me* to hand-wash it and to use some bleach and warm water. I did so because I was told to do it, but my hands are now burning because there are no latex or rubber gloves here. If bleach splashed on my clothing, I am going to be *ultra-pissed*, as well. I have no funds to replace clothing... and what I have on was new three weeks ago.

I hate this job more with every passing moment. At least when I was bullied in a law firm, I was compensated for the disrespect.

Asking for More and Taking More Away

Two days ago, I was told that I have to be here for Christmas. I cannot have the holiday to spend with my son and I am expected to prepare the family meal (for ten people): to serve and clean up afterward. I cannot see Mattie for Christmas, and we cannot see a new movie release on Christmas day, which has been our family tradition now for years. We look forward to that holiday structure, every single year. This year is even more important because I am here with him "in his city."

I HATE being obliged to spend CHRISTMAS here. I do not celebrate Christmas, and I am angry that they are forcing me to do so. Yet, I keep that inside my head.

I made one last attempt at companionship/social interaction with Roxanne around 7:50 PM this evening. I had to remove my eyeglasses to clean them, then put them back onto my shirt to hang; she asked me to look at something, and I put them on again, then she said with a rather rude laugh, "I wish you would decide what you're doing with those damned glasses." I looked her in the eye, got up, and walked away. I didn't
return until 8:20 PM, telling her it then was time to go to bed.

I performed all the usual duties: emptied the commode and inserted a new bag, tidied her bathroom, and removed her hearing aid (she again tried to insist I open the hearing aid. I have no nails (which she also criticizes regularly) and could not open the device. Even with my eyeglasses, I could not see how to open the hearing aid. I returned it to her, and she opened it effortlessly. She can open her own hearing aid but has determined I am her slave labor and continues to ask more and more of me for the same nominal compensation.

I considered the hell there would be to pay if I had opened the device and damaged it. I suppose that was an ulterior motive in the mix for her. They could then refuse to pay me and keep me imprisoned for manual labor until I had contributed the money it took to replace the device. Not today, Roxanne. Not tomorrow, either.

I am rather in awe of the absurdity of her bullying, judgment, and disrespect — yet all the while, demanding more and more.

DECEMBER 13, 2016

It sure didn't take long for the honeymoon to be short-circuited. Today, Dolores suggested she would bring down some logs, give me an ax, and have me split kindling.

I refused, and I smiled and asked her if she wanted to see a copy of her advert for the position. My next step would be to be direct in reminding her they had requested this and many other newly added tasks for me — for the same remuneration as the basic tasks.

She walked away angry but said nothing. I presume she realized she had just *tried* and failed, but she already knew she was operating on a manipulative whim. These two women are assuredly members of the "give an inch, take three miles" club.

The infamous wood stove of Hell House

DECEMBER 14, 2016

I was up at 4:30 this morning and watched Netflix on my computer in my room until 5:30. Despite trying to take ownership of anything in this scenario that might be on *my* shoulders, I reconsidered the increasing duties I am asked to perform here versus the pay I am accommodated for it. The following is what I did for Roxanne yesterday.

1. Let Sophie out
2. Fed Sophie
3. Made coffee
4. Baked a cake
5. Set out Roxanne's meds & 2 juices
6. Sophie whining; made her go out again; NOTED SHE HAD POOPED ON THE FLOOR in front of the stereo (dry, easy clean up; she must have done this yesterday, as I vacuumed in the early morning; I let her out eight times (yes, I counted) yesterday, but I think she does not want to go out in the cold; I let Dolores know, worrying that Dolores will merely tell me to get it done — after all, Sophie is a little poodle — I am a grown woman and the local slave labor.
7. Set out porridge for microwave warm-up
8. Started a fire in the woodstove
9. Swept the back ramp; applied de-icer
10. Swept the front porch; applied de-icer

11. Swept the back porch

12. 7:50 – Roxanne rang to get up; gave her hearing aid, brushed teeth, provided her eyeglasses (I had cleaned them in advance); wet face cloth

13. Roxanne was in a bad mood/grumpy; she demanded I clean her eyeglasses and handed them back to me; I told her I would clean them again; I did so. She said "thank *YOU*," grumpy-style — as though she had been commanded to say thank you to her servant. I note Dolores is well aware of how her mother treats me.

14. Roxanne scolded me for not taking her through physio exercises yesterday; I said I would only do those when she asked for it/felt like doing them; she told me Dolores wanted those done every day (that was news to me, as Dolores had never written such instructions or instructed me verbally); we performed two sets of three different exercises

15. Assisted Roxanne to the commode, combed her hair, and changed her clothes (she refused to have a new undershirt; asked me to clip her monitor higher; she was very grumpy & demanding)

16. Wheeled Roxanne into the kitchen; provided coffee & porridge; provided 2nd cup of coffee

17. 9 AM, Roxanne demanded more coffee (still grumpy); I mentioned I would make more and that it would only take a minute; she responded, "Just make me tea" — I made tea

18. Dolores brought down kindling & Lemon Lysol

19. Brought in two buckets of wood from outside; stacked those neatly inside

20. I stacked kindling outdoors because Dolores brought more wood down to her mother's property and dumped it in disarray outside as she has started doing regularly

10 AM

1. Watered the plants

2. Changed bed linens

3. Did two loads of laundry, dried, folded & put away

4. Took Roxanne to commode; emptied & changed bag; still grumpy

11:30 AM

1. Swept the three porches again (light snow removal)

2. Got Roxanne's lunch ready (she asked for a small piece of cake before lunch; I gave it to her (despite this being taboo, per Dolores' instructions; I am simply tired of the banter and conflict); I warmed her tea, but she is still grumpy)

3. I let Sophie out, but had to go outside to pick her up; she was crying and her feet were in pain from the frigid snow; I dried

her off with a towel and she was fine then — running around "puppy style" for three rounds (not in any arthritic pain as Roxanne invariably attests)

4. I restoked the fire

2 PM

1. Pre-prepped Brussel sprouts & scalloped potatoes

2. Took Roxanne back for a nap (emptied commode; changed bag); helped Roxanne into bed (she needs a push every time now; she is unable to

transition from the side of her bed to 12″ from the edge by herself (or so she claims now — she was doing that just fine until about three days ago)

3. Sophie out (no issues)

4. Restoked the fire

4:15 PM

1. Roxanne rang early; wanted to go through physio exercises; did two sets of three different exercises

2. Commode emptied and fresh bag inserted

3. Made tea for Roxanne

4. Prepared salmon (crusted with orange peel, lemon pepper & drizzled with Bearnaise sauce); sides of Brussel sprouts & scalloped potatoes

5. 5 PM: dinner served she did not eat all the Brussel sprouts (she gave the balance to Sophie); dessert was rice pudding & cake (chocolate with huckleberries, sunflower seeds & cranberries)

6. Washed & dried & put away dishes; placed left-over food into containers & labeled

7. Sophie out and gave her a meal after

8. Re-stoked the fire

9. Made more tea for Roxanne

10. Provided dessert: rice pudding & cake

7:30 PM (Dolores visited & delivered my payroll so I would have it tomorrow on my day off)

1. Performed Roxanne's blood work

2. Provided a snack (rice pudding)

7:50 PM

1. Asked Roxanne if she wanted her tea. "Warm it up" (I did)

2. 8:05 PM – asked Roxanne to retire to the bedroom for reading; she again refused, snapping, "Can't you see I'm still reading? What are you going to do about it?"

3. 8:15 PM – she ignored me as I stood to wheel her back to her bedroom

4. 8:20 PM – I returned; she begrudgingly put down her book, and I took her to the bedroom

5. Commode (cleaned, & inserted new bag); helped Roxanne into the bed (she needs a push every time now; seemingly cannot transition from the side of the bed to 12″ from the edge by herself)

6. She asked for her pillow to be adjusted three times, very demanding, and very grumpy. It visibly irritated me, and she looked at me and challenged, "*What*?"

I replied, "I'm just tired."

She snarled, "I *know* you're tired."

Me, exhausted

7. I removed her eyeglasses and turned out her lights at 9:20 PM.

I wish she would cooperate to transition to reading in her room promptly at 8 PM, as Dolores mandates. By this time, I need to sit down and recuperate. I am still adjusting to staying awake until 9:30 PM when I turn out her lights. My typical bedtime, for years now, has been 8 or 8:30 PM, keeping the same schedule as my son.

Well, I pat myself on the back for enduring still another turmoil of a day. Tomorrow will assuredly be a better day. I see my Mattie!

STRATEGIZED ENTRAPMENT

It's mid-December now — December 15th. The days pass very slowly here, but TODAY — I have almost 48 hours with my Mattie!

Earlier today, in the sunshine... he tells me, "At least it's warmer now."

"Buddy, it's minus ten degrees!"

Then, ten minutes ago, he tells me "Told 'ya it was warmer before. It's minus 24 now!"

"Summer's around the corner — don't worry!"

"Mom, are you okay?"

Yesterday was not what we would call a good day; Roxanne was much more congenial when Dolores was here; other than that, she was very grumpy, demanding more and more in her continuing rude tone. She is well aware of what she is doing. I do not know why, as she has to recognize her history with caregivers here and that she is also now pushing *me* over the edge. I will not tolerate feeling bullied, having more and more tasks expected/demanded of me, and being unappreciated (there is never a thank you other than the GRUMPY, curt "thank YOU," as though I've done what is expected of me; no appreciation for the extras in presentation or food preparation [I plan to give her a plain, boring meal on my next workday, and see if anything is noticed; if not, I will no longer bother with the extras; it merely makes more work for me and if it is not appreciated, I do not want to endure that).

It's clear now that the job will not work for me. I will commit (solely to myself) to staying through March, but if nothing has changed, I will probably return to work in legal and move into the city. Finding I am wearing down fast and losing my patience, I hide it less and less with both Roxanne *and* Dolores. Once I have had enough, and my tolerance level is waning, I allow some of my facial expressions to shine through and cease giving any verbal response (as I do not want to disrespect her or respond unprofessionally). I'm confident that she thinks she has "won" the debate with this response, and I am happy to let her think that — simply to avoid more unnecessary conflict and melodrama.

The physio exercises that are now demanded of me, the earlier arising in the morning, the earlier arising from her nap time, and then later transferring to bed all seem to be purposeful items for "pushing me" — to see how much I can or will take.

I am stunned; does she think this is such a profoundly excellent job that I will not leave? Or, does she think me incapable of doing anything better, simply because I kowtow to her every whim?

Yesterday she also asked me why I color my hair; I told her to have it white would make me look older, and in my profession in legal, no one hires an elderly woman for the job; it was necessary to appear younger and also that I take pride in my appearance (too many digs on my hair, my nails, that I don't need to put any lotions on my skin, that I don't need to exercise — that it is peculiar). I feel as though she wants me to wither and appear unconditioned, to be trapped here. Does she not understand that if I cannot keep myself healthy & conditioned, I cannot care for her?

I recognize more, with every passing day, that this is very unhealthy for me... I am wearing down on a different level than I did working in law firms. NEITHER is good, NEITHER can be acceptable, one over the other. One pays $9,600 per year and the other pays $75,000. Hmmm. It doesn't take a rocket scientist to figure out that suffering can be considered with a better price tag.

Today, I started a document entitled "Care Log." My background in law tells me to be prepared in case the "bottom falls out" of this strategized entrapment they've executed on me.

Melodrama and Nightmares

Yesterday, I had problems with Roxanne. At 9:45 AM yesterday, another one of Roxanne's daughters phoned. I handed her the telephone, but she took too long to answer it. She tried to return the call but could not get the number right. While she struggled to find the number in one of her old phone books; I asked her why she didn't want to use the phone book I made for her; she said (in that insolent tone with which she is so expert), "Cause I can't REACH it."

I told her, "That's where you *told* me to put it." She continued to struggle to find the number in the three older, poorly documented books. I asked her jokingly (to break the ice) if I had wasted my time creating that new phone book for her and she snapped and raised her voice, "Don't get snitty with me."

In a soft, polite tone of voice, I told her, "Well, if you are snitty with me, you cannot expect me to sit here and be peachy and sweet; I will just leave the room. I will not be bullied, Roxanne."

She argued she was *not* being rude, and I replied (with a chuckle, careful to ensure it was not a rude one) that maybe we should have a tape recorder. She snapped again, telling me not to be rude. I then told her, "If you are not happy with me here, all you have to do is let me know."

She then calmed down and meekly said, "Don't be silly."

"I'm serious as a heart attack, Roxanne," adding a quiet smile. I clarified I would not argue with her, but I would also not be bullied. "Everybody, including me, works hard here to keep you comfortable and tries to improve your life. If it is not good enough, you need to let me know, because I cannot do any more than I am already doing." I have observed that the more I do in the household, the more I am asked to do. Talk about another learning curve.

I have had nightmares over the past two consecutive nights. Two nights, my dream had me crawling through a large drainage pipe; I was running from something or someone and could only move forward — not knowing where the pipe would emerge or what would be on the other side greeting me.: It has now faded, but I wrote in my journal on awakening. Last night, I dreamed I was being held captive. I was escaping and trying to carry all my clothes and shoes, and kept dropping things. On my way to render an apology in a boardroom meeting with a female lawyer for whom I worked in the past, I had a feeling I would receive something in return... I was to render the apology in Japanese because others had said I did not speak the language as I attested — those who spoke *some* Japanese said mine made little sense (I used the formal Japanese I had learned in University). Not wanting to be ostracized, criticized, and bullied again, I opted to bypass the meeting. I kept dropping my clothes; I did not know where I was going. This was full-scale, fight or flight. My poor amygdala — working overtime these past couple of weeks. I woke up.

I surmise the meaning of that dream is that I do feel trapped and imprisoned. It is now 6:15 AM. Thankfully, the dog is not up yet. I feel I am losing myself. I hate it here, but I must stay until I have money to leave — to escape.

PRELUDE TO BREAKING POINT

Time to wash my face, brush my teeth, make coffee and start another fire, begin another day, feed the dog, and let her outside... I will not see Mattie until Friday. I feel this will be an endless week. I will have Friday and Saturday off. Christmas Day is Sunday; I am grateful they finally gave permission for him to be here with me, but I do not have the freedom to do what I want with him on Christmas Day. Dolores told me yesterday, "You can bring him here for Christmas Day and he can spend the night — but he will have to stay in your room and keep himself occupied. He'll be in the way here. You're going to be very busy." She said it in such a tone as to imply she was granting me *excessive accommodation* for the inconvenience.

And he will have to watch me in a position of servitude with these people. I have concerns that Dolores and Roxanne will exhibit their true natures — and I would really not want Matthew to see that, anyway. I hate being here all the more because of this.

Mattie only wants to spend time with me — to be *near* me. And he does not want to spend Christmas at the group home.

Reflections on a Sunday morning? Happy to be in Kamloops, and happy to see my son once a week. But alas, despite my diligent efforts, I cannot find humor or positivity in every situation. Life just doesn't roll like that, here at Hell House.

The caregiver-housekeeping position is a living nightmare, worsening with each passing day. True colors emerged from the patient at week 2.5. She is rude, belittling, unappreciative, bullying, demands more duties from me *daily*, and I tolerate insults with no apology unless her daughter forces her to apologize.

I have had to engage professional boundaries, NO to shoveling driveways, NO to grooming the dog, NO to trimming the dog's toenails, NO to grooming the dog's badly matted fur, NO to chopping wood, and so very much more. At every turn, I have performed some extra duties beyond what they initially outlined as the duties for my position. After all, that is *my modus operandi* — my usual work-ethic presentation, but all has been thankless or has produced insults and comments about how I could do more. I am worn thin, hardly sleeping and when I do, I awaken from nightmares... I feel imprisoned. Every morning, I find myself annoyed with the premise of daylight and dreading the day ahead of me.

My Mattie's voice rings in my ears, "Sleep is my peace." Yes, buddy — I sure get that.

Fortunately, I keep a personal journal and detailed care log each day, comprehensively documenting everything. I have an itemized list of duties for which they hired me (job description), and I am already performing at least double what they initially outlined. I have gently expressed limits and boundaries, but I am approaching a breaking point now that I predict will see my assertion skills rise to the calling.

I continue to be insulted daily, and when I give my time over and above to make Roxanne's life more enjoyable, or easier, I am met with demands for more. Today, she even told me I am wasting my time with what I have done! I continue to do only that which was confirmed as part of my job description when hired, but I perform all duties with impeccable pride. My grandfather taught me six decades ago, "Autograph your work with excellence and always leave a workplace better than you found it."

When my son was here last, it appalled him to see how I am treated here. He is worried about my physical and mental health. I truly tried to avoid having him witness the turmoil here; it is not good for him, since he is so sensitive and empathetic — and loves me *so very much*.

I will remain here no longer than March 2017 and will deliberate my options in the three months I have left.

Ten years from now, I want to make sure I can say that I CHOSE my life, and did not settle for it. I made this venture closer to my son, and I have learned immensely from the experiences. I am certain I will learn more — even if it is only to appreciate my freedom, as I do not have it over five days in a 24-hour shift here. When we make a choice, we also choose the consequences.

DECEMBER 19, 2016

Dolores saw I was about to collapse last night, and sent me to bed at 6:30. I had been through too much on the job and she could see I was wearing thin. She gave me two "222" tablets to help me sleep, and I took them. She told me she would manage her mother this evening.

She added they do not want to see me leave, that I am appreciated and needed here. She knows this has gone too far.

I am grateful for the rest, grateful for her affirmation that things had not been good — but I will not take more bait. Any option of remaining here beyond Spring 2017 does not exist. I will continue to provide my utmost until that time, but I have to take care of myself before I can adequately take care of anyone else... If my health declines, how could I ever explain to Mattie that I let myself run off the tracks for a *stranger*?

Today was a slightly better day, but I cannot trust Roxanne in any capacity.

Case in point, her son Robert & his wife visited with Kentucky Fried Chicken dinner supplies. I opted out; Darlene & Dave were fine with that.

At dinner, I heard Roxanne tell them the two butter tarts in the kitchen disappeared, insinuating I had eaten them! Sauntering into the kitchen and jokingly (but seriously) I said, "Hey you had one butter tart with ice cream at lunch, and also rice pudding at lunch." I said nothing more, and Dolores laughed! I feel no sense of loyalty to Roxanne; I am here to do her daughter's bidding as a housekeeper, cook, and caregiver, no more — no less.

Robert spoke with me privately in the kitchen. "Thank you for taking care of my mother."

"It's my job." I smiled politely. He asked if there were problems, and I hesitated but responded honestly, "Yes, there are problems. But Dolores is on that. I understand your mother's frustrations with losing her freedom and her independence, her sense of autonomy, and her ability to be active. If it were me, I would likely be worse; I would be very indignant and bitter, I'm sure."

He thanked me again. Later, he returned to speak with me when saying goodbye, adding I was more than welcome to sit with them the next time they came. I thanked him but told him, "Ahh, I prefer to keep business as *business* and to maintain professional boundaries. No offence intended, but that's what is best for me."

He said he understood. I don't care if he did or didn't; this is temporary.

Before Dolores left, I wanted to view Roxanne's emails, to see what I had sent her; she was snippy. Of course, she is being called to task in front of her daughter this time. She snapped, "Open one. Do what you wanna do. You're gonna do it, anyway." Lovely — that sure makes me want to do more?

Dolores tried four times to prompt her to say please, and Roxanne emphatically refused. Softly I remarked, "I won't send any more. I only sent emails because you complained, and I quote, your exact words to me were that 'no one cared or thought about' you. I suspect I did not need to elaborate directly that my reasoning was that additional attention was (1) not appreciated, (2) was expected, now and (3) made more work and negative interaction for me with Roxanne.

Opportunity to learn, Roxanne: be careful when shooting your messenger in the foot.

Robert and his wife left, and Dave and Dolores returned up the hill. Because Roxanne was in a mood, I left her to read, checking on her tea from time to time. I transferred her down to her room at 8:15. She was still belligerent, so I did not engage. Once in her room, she was more dramatic, more demanding than ever. I complied and ignored the antics. She did not even try to reach for the lower support rope there to assist her in her self-transfer. Rather, she insisted I place it in her hand. I did. She insisted I move the blankets back. "Move 'em back more — ALL the way back — listen to me and do what I say!" When I did, the tray on her bed and all its contents went over the other side, onto the floor behind the bed.

"NOW, what have you done?" she snapped. I picked up the tray and all items and returned them to the top of her bed. She made no effort to push herself over in the bed, insisting I *move her over*. I did and asked, "So, are you set?" When she ignored me and began reading her book, I left her to her reading, adding that I would return around 9:30 to turn out her lights.

At 9:40, I returned to turn out her lights. She did not want to go to sleep, but she cooperated. I said goodnight.

At 9:45 she *shouted* for me, rather than ringing her bell. I went down the hall, turned on her light, and she commanded me to put her leg warmers on — "those striped ones." I did. She said, "Thank *YOU*" in her demanding tone (as though to imply I was her slave and had completed my instructions at her behest). I am extremely uncomfortable with these interactions.

DECEMBER 20, 2016

At 10 today, "Bath Girl" Cody comes in. I will need to leave the premises likely, as I despise the way she puts me down and makes random, unjustified, and unsubstantiated criticism. I do, however, suspect Roxanne starts the conversation. Roxanne complains about all caregivers in some capacity. She has had negatives to relate in response to every other caregiver that has ever been here. I have learned, however, through Dolores, that Roxanne has used the same demanding, snarky tone with others — and they would not tolerate it; they all left — most abruptly, without notice. I left, took my car, and got some gas.

When I returned and the fire was getting low (Cody was giving Roxanne her bath), I added another log. Sophie wanted to go outside, and I let her out — and back inside again when she barked. Despite these things being *Cody's* responsibilities, for which she is paid about $25/hour, I accommodated and then returned to my room, out of confrontation's way. I have remained in my room with the door closed the entire time she was here. Once again, I felt I could not go into the kitchen to have my lunch. **This is grossly unacceptable.** I hope Dolores complains to the health authority and has them send another care aide. Otherwise, this repeating childish game-playing will assuredly hasten my departure.

At 1:30, I had one of Matt's cigarettes; I keep an emergency supply for him here, as the home has been negligent in sending him out with his allocated supply for a day with me. I had to get away from the house. PTSD was about to cripple me and I worried about what might slip from my mouth… I ventured up the hill and visited with Dave, Dolores' husband — who was already outside shoveling snow.

I am in awe of Dave, actually — to live with the melodrama that has haunted this property for decades and still be one of the kindest, calmest individuals I have ever met? It's nothing short of remarkable. He is a joy to be around.

Dave invited me into the house, a big post-modern wood and glass home with well-chosen appointments. He gave me a tour of the house, then made me a cup of tea and I explained what had transpired — and how I could not endure much more. He gave me a detailed rendition of ugly family history, which provided me with sufficient background to discern that these two women did this to *everyone*, and not just to me.

He told me not to worry about the event, to come back if I needed to, and he assured me that Dolores would deal with this when she got home. I walked back down the hill to the shoddy dilapidated trailer that is Hell House.

By 2:30, I was in a full-blown PTSD response, complete with chest pains, atrial fibrillation, and tremors, making me shake like I was having a mild seizure. Then the tears came.

Roxanne rang her bell around 3:30. I had to stop my abrupt crying and "straighten up." I performed her usual duties. She knew I was quite upset. She said nothing, and neither did I.

Around 4 PM, the health authority telephoned, wanting my version of events with Bath Girl. I complied. I tried to reach Dolores by cell phone but she had not taken her phone with her. She was out making her weekly egg deliveries to clients in the city. I telephoned Dave, and he said not to worry.

Dolores arrived around 7 PM. I regurgitated the sequence of events; she said she would phone the health authority in the morning.

Tonight, I prepared pork tenderloin, potatoes, and carrots for Roxanne. She did not touch her vegetables, but she had two desserts. I have given up on trying to insist on Dolores' protocols at mealtime (e.g., no dinner/no dessert if dinner). I prefer to avoid the conflict and focus on keeping Roxanne assuaged.

I could barely keep myself awake to turn out Roxanne's light at the usual time. I felt ill — sick-exhausted. I slept with no medication but woke up about six times through the night — wide awake by 5 AM.

Great advice this morning from a trusted friend. "If your client is behaving like a child, why would you treat her like an adult?" The bottom line, she is fully aware of the abuse and manipulation tactics she exhibits more profoundly with each passing day. There is no dementia there; Roxanne is perceptive and purposeful. Frequently, she has shown that she is well familiar with and capable of performing tasks she insists on having me perform for her. She wants a servant. She enjoys exercising power.

I will try opting for alternative responses to her derision, insults, and abuse, including not actively responding to these manipulation tactics with anger. I will do my best to cease enabling, as though I were dealing with a child.

Today is another day. I will control what I can and attempt to ignore the rest. My reprieve will come in the Spring.

Guess that's hope and faith personified — hope for the future being different and faith that I can survive until that time.

4 AM

Krikey. I did not sleep well, despite 2-1/2 222 tablets. I can't get past feeling like Roxanne's slave. She has become more impertinent, more demanding, and inordinately unpleasant when Dolores is not present. I have become PTSD-triggered, again.

This morning, I provided her breakfast — and given it is quite cold outside, I asked if she wanted a warm beanbag for her hip and she said "Yes, please."

PLEASE? Wow! That stopped me in my tracks! I accommodated.

She tried looking at her emails but had no new ones since yesterday. In a high-pitched, whining tone she told me "No one cares about me; no one thinks about me."

I mentioned it was the holiday season and people were busy shopping and preparing. I sent her a few emails, trying to lift her spirits. But, foolish me: I broke my own rule — I did extra. Of course, it *backfired on me.*

Within minutes, she demanded I open the emails for her and read them to her. She complained when her iPad did not open swiftly. "I can see *you* sent these to me. What the hell do they say and why won't they open fast? Do you even know what you are doing?"

She also pretends to not understand how to access her emails; I have taught her this lesson six times, and I now recognize she does anything to manipulate me to do more for her. Anything. I watched her open emails this morning, without prompting — only to tell me there was nothing new there. She revisited her emails received yesterday on her own accord. Again, she is fully capable. She is simply manipulating.

Then, as I am washing dishes while she eats her breakfast, she demands I return to her table and hand her a fork. The fork is easily within her reach. She also snapped, "While you're at it — refill my water. I don't want to bother with it myself."

Lesson learned now, I hope. I will reduce my personal interaction with her from this point forward; I give up. If I do not, I will not survive this. Nightmares, sleeplessness, tremors from anxiety — there is nothing good for my mental or physical health in this position. When we make a choice, we also choose the consequences. I sure find myself in a web of sticky predicaments again.

DECEMBER 21, 2016

Roxanne did not arise early today. Per the protocols in place from Dolores, I woke her up at 8:15. She was exhausted, but not in a bad mood. I kept things to a "usual" breakfast and "usual" duties. Nothing more/nothing less.

Dolores visited in the morning. She advised that Cody, *aka "Bath Girl,"* would not be returning. She added she had asked *not to return*, telling the health authority that she enjoyed working with "Gramma" but would not return because of me.

Gaslighting at its finest: Bath Girl does a crappy job, doesn't show any work ethic, makes trouble and drama at every turn... and now, doesn't want the job anymore because of me, on my day off! What a preposterous nightmare!

A VERY BAD revisiting of events transpired after that. Dolores accused me of slamming a door (those were Cody's words), though she stated I was *almost* blameless. That was it. There was the official breaking point.

I disclosed information I had never confided until now, wanting to avoid conflict and just move past this absurd scenario. "I guess you were never told that Bath Girl knocked on my closed bedroom door and *opened it*, **stepped into my private room unannounced**, solely to spark confrontation! Cody, the twenty-something Bath Girl, told me, "You might want to put less wood on that fire — it's way too hot in here."

My only communication to her, as I stepped within six inches of her, causing her to back up and exit my room, was, "I do not take instructions from you. We take our instructions from the family. Our jobs do not intertwine. You do you, and I'll do me." And with that, I gently closed my bedroom door. *Gently*. Purposefully. With premeditated intention.

I exploded to Dolores. Gloves were *off*. I told her I did not slam any fucking door and I am 100 percent blameless. I used the "F" bomb several times; I did not care. She told me to calm down, and I told her I would not — I would not take any more of this abuse and rhetoric. I stormed out to have another one of Matt's cigarettes (yes; I keep a supply here for him in case the group home fails to provide adequately for him when he leaves for his visitation). Dolores followed me outside.

She apologized, and I repeated, not disguising my rage, insisting I did not slam a door — I closed the door gently and did so *purposefully*. I am BLAMELESS in this scenario. "Let me tell you — if I had *chosen* to slam a door, you can bet money neither of us has that door would be off the hinges right now and your neighbors a block away would have heard it. No exaggeration. I did not even SEE this idiot Bath Girl from the time she came in; I never engaged her; I never left my ROOM. I stayed in my room to hide from her and to avoid the confrontation that I *knew* was coming." I reminded her that "part of my job working in law involved profiling skills — and my letters of reference will confirm my proficiency with that."

I did not let Dolores get a word in edge-wise. "Further, I did not eat between 7:30 AM and 2 PM, to AVOID going into the kitchen. All of this was grossly unacceptable. I am not slave labor to be abused, ridiculed, and falsely accused." I was livid. She had never seen me angry, and she had never heard me use profanity,

of course. Both of them had only seen me kowtow, remain kind and patient —
but ultimately refuse additional duties imposed.

She apologized again. I repeated myself and smoked the cigarette. I made no
effort to keep the smoke away from her face. After all, she followed me out here.
She said that *she* had embellished by saying I had slammed the door, adding she
was wrong to do so. *Ya think?*

She apologized again, and asked me to forgive her, adding, "We should just put
this behind us." I was not inclined to express forgiveness. I have far too much
experience with personalities like these two women here. You forgive, you get
stepped on again. After all, Frick and Frack from the Surrey law firm were my most
profound of teachers.

I told her I did not leave a career that paid me $75K per annum to be treated like
this. "I moved here for peace, and to make a person in their final years of life better.
This has turned out to be the antithesis of peace. I refuse to be triggered to illness,
worn down repeatedly, and needlessly disparaged." I never told her I accepted her
apology — because I didn't. And I certainly never said I forgave her.

She told me she was very happy with the job I was doing, and she needed me
here. Of course, she is — of course, she *does*. My work ethic has been impeccable.

I said nothing, refusing to continue a circular argument or dignify the foolish
manipulation with a response.

Dolores came to see Roxanne at 5:50 PM, to go over her monthly accounting.
She asked me if I was feeling better — as though all should be fine now. I told her
I was sick, that this invariably happened after a confrontation event, but it would
pass. She asked if Gravol would help, and I told her no, just needed calm and time.
"You're a nurse — this is not motion sickness; this is PTSD triggering a physical
health response."

I told her it would pass and I would be fine by morning, but the unnecessary
conflict, discourtesy, and mockery cannot continue.

I did not maintain my care log today; I was just too exhausted and utterly
drained. I napped while Roxanne was down for *her* nap — sleeping with my door
open, of course, so I could hear her ring from her room when she awakened.

By 5:15, she was still snoring in her room, and I had to get her up for dinner,
which was a basic meal of mashed potatoes, steamed green beans, gravy, and a
hamburger patty. She picked at the meal and ate perhaps 25 percent of it. She asked
for dessert, and despite that going against Dolores' commandments, I complied. I
gave her homemade chocolate cake, with 1 sliced strawberry and some vanilla ice
cream.

As any child would do, she ate it all, in between nodding out at the dinner table.

I am absolutely *stir crazy* and miserable here. I said before that I hate it more with
every passing day — but alas, that was a dishonest representation. After all, nobody

likes a complain-freak. More accurately, I hate it here, more and more, with every passing *minute*. All I can think about to make myself happier/less miserable is to envision leaving — having my independence again, having my personal space, no matter how small... I want my freedom and my privacy again. I want to choose the foods I will eat. I want to go to bed at 8 PM if I am so inclined.

I cannot help but feel this is some sort of distorted nightmare from which I will awaken hyperventilating and in a cold sweat... But no, this is reality. It's my "circus reality" at the moment, for having accepted a job in desperation to be closer to my son... I believe in taking ownership, and this is assuredly "on me." Now, I reap the consequences of a rapid-fire decision made.

January will mark my time for aggressively seeking alternate employment. For now, I smile and move forward, knowing I am responsible for my response and for my future... and for now, I will count the seconds until I see my son on Friday morning! And February should see the arrival of my income tax return — funding for freedom. Independence money!

Bottom line, I survived what will now be known as "Turd Tuesday." Yes, it was "the *shitz*," but not the "*shiznit*!"

THE ONLY WAY UP... IS OUT

Today is December 22.

Bad sleep last night with my mind working overtime, reliving the past two days and the melodrama that triggered my PTSD response. I've been wide awake since 2:30 AM, and at 3 AM, I took a 222, but to no avail. These women have me taking a mild narcotic — something that has always gone against my health protocols.

Heck, two days ago, Roxanne critically asked me, in that infamous surly tone of hers, "Why don't you eat desserts? I see you eat a bite of ice cream now and then, but you make all these cakes, and pies, and muffins, and you don't eat any of it. Why? They're good enough for me but not good enough for *you?*"

"I recently had some blood work come back, warming me I was pre-diabetes. Thus, I decreased my sugar intake by about 98 percent. I could never afford the cost of insulin if I became diabetic. My first financial commitments are to my son; I prefer to keep my health on track and be minimalist in what I have."

"Well, that's just stupid. Eat your cake and enjoy your life. Even if you are diabetic, they don't put you on insulin right away; first, you start with pills and Pharmacare covers those. Eat what you want. Stop being stupid. I really don't understand your nonsense."

It's now 7:13 AM, and I've had my shower, washed my hair, moisturized my face (oh, Roxanne would be displeased with that), and changed clothes. Now, it's time to begin another day at Hell House, letting the dog out, starting the fire, setting out Roxanne's breakfast, juices (one small unsweetened cranberry, one shot of apple cider vinegar, all Dolores protocols), and medication — then, I'm ready to awaken her for her day to begin at 8 AM. She goes to get her hair cut this morning and to see her doctor. I will change bed linens and do laundry while she is gone.

Because these women seem to think I am paid well enough ($800 per month for 24-7 service accommodation 5.5 days per week), and because they continue to add more duties to my already long day, I again itemized all I have done.

1. Watered plants; changed bed linens; brought in two buckets of wood from outside; stacked one inside
2. Added five logs to the fire by 10 AM
3. Did two loads of laundry, folded and put it all away
4. Made date squares while Roxanne was at the doctor's office
5. Brought in more wood
6. Did the third load of laundry
7. When Dolores returned, I helped her up the stairs with the wheelchair, cleaned the snow/de-icer off the floors that she tracked in, and ran the vacuum on the rugs in the mudroom
8. Roxanne had her vitamins and some yogurt.

When I was putting her down for her nap (3:15), she asked what she could get me for Christmas. I asked her to please not get me anything, as I hated Christmas. She pressed me to elaborate. I told her again (I've told her before) that my mother told me I was disinherited on Christmas day 37 years ago. I have hated the holiday ever since. For 20 years, Matt and I have seen a movie on Christmas day, that is all I wanted to do, but I am refused the day off. I am forced to stay here. She told me I could go see a movie another day.

"Next year, I will take Mattie to a movie. This will not happen to us again."

"What? I will still be here."

I told her she would likely be in Gemstone by then. Then she pressed, "Does Dolores know you're not staying?"

"Roxanne, this is not an appropriate conversation."

She pressed, and I told her I was sure Dolores knew this was not a forever position for me. I cannot wash my car, I cannot do anything but pay my bills and even those run short. I cannot do anything for my son. Before Christmas next year, I will have to return to my career. I repeated this was not the time to have this conversation.

GOOD GRIEF, I am sick of the senseless melodrama here. I am sick *all over again,* and I am experiencing tremors again, too.

And despite my efforts to redirect myself repeatedly, I am again PISSED OFF that I am forced to work Christmas Day and *forced* to sit down and have a fucking Christmas Dinner with these people. THAT is not business. I HATE THIS with every breath in my body.

When Dolores was here this afternoon (before Roxanne went down for her nap), she mentioned I could take the time to drive into Wal-Mart now, rather than in the morning. I said thanks, but I wanted to keep schedules as business, clear-cut and separate. She said, "Well, you're going to be cooking in here on your day off, on Saturday!"

"NO, I won't be — not on my day off. I will cook on Christmas Day, but not on my day off." I could not tell whether she was seeing how far she could push me, but I was *not* taking this bait. She said nothing. Nice try, Chickie; not this time. You have mistaken my willingness to help for weakness to be exploited. I told myself, "She *really* does not know who or what I am."

She continues to repeat manipulative, insincere comments such as, "This is your home; we want you to feel this is your home."

Save that for someone who might need to hear it. This is not my home; this is my prison and learning opportunity. My décor is not my own, my food choices are not my own. My time is not my own 5.5 days over a 24-hour responsibility commitment. She also keeps repeating comments like "We want you to consider us family — that's why we want you at Christmas dinner."

Tell that to some fool who might believe you, woman: you want me here because Christmas dinner for 10 people is a *whack* of a lot of work, as is setting a dinner table, serving, and cleaning up when everyone has had their fill. I am not family and never WILL be family. This is a slave-labor, excruciatingly underpaid HARD-WORK job. And I will hate all this all the more for being forced to be here on friggin' Christmas day.

GOOD GRIEF, I am sick of the senseless melodrama here. I am sick *all over again,* and I am experiencing tremors again, too.

And despite having redirected my thoughts repeatedly, I am again PISSED OFF that I am forced to work Christmas Day and *forced* to sit down and have a fucking Christmas Dinner with these people. THAT is not business. I HATE THIS with every breath in my body.

When Dolores was here this afternoon (before Roxanne went down for her nap), she mentioned I could take the time to drive into Wal-Mart now, rather than in the morning. I said thanks, but I wanted to keep schedules as business, clear-cut and separate. She said, "Well, you're going to be cooking in here on your day off, on Saturday!"

"NO, I won't be — not on my day off. I will cook on Christmas Day, but not on my day off." I could not tell whether she was seeing how far she could push me, but I was *not* taking this bait. She said nothing. Nice try, Chickie; not this time.

She keeps repeating manipulative, insincere comments like, "This is your home; we want you to feel this is your home."

This is not my home; this is my prison and learning opportunity. My décor is not my own, my food choices are not my own. My time is not my own 5.5 days over a 24-hour responsibility commitment. She also keeps repeating comments like "We want you to consider us family — that's why we want you at Christmas dinner."

Tell that to some fool who might believe you, woman: you want me here because Christmas dinner for 10 people is a *whack* of a lot of work, as is setting a dinner table, serving, and cleaning up when everyone has had their fill. I am not family and never WILL be family. This is a slave-labor, excruciatingly underpaid HARD-WORK job. And I will hate all this all the more for being forced to be here on friggin' Christmas day.

I miss my Mattie *so much*.

DECEMBER 23, 2016

More issues with the group home. It's a really good thing that Matthew is unaware of how badly things are faring for me here. I have kept about 99 percent of that from him. My email to the group home manager is below.

> Matt has advised me that, as of yesterday, his daily allowable cigarette intake was increased from eight cigarettes (plan in place for five consecutive years now, successfully) to ten cigarettes.

> I ask that you discontinue this increase immediately. This is not in the interests of Matt's health in any capacity; it increases his need (addiction) for more nicotine and prevents him from ever being hopeful of decreasing or ultimately quitting, and he cannot afford to smoke more. He has learned discipline on the eight-cigarette-per-day plan over the years and this increase is a shocking change, not in his best interests. When Matt smoked more than eight cigarettes per day in the past, his addition-relative behaviours changed.

> If he has misunderstood the increase to ten cigarettes per day, I also ask that you advise me, as his Committee of person and estate. This is a life-altering decision involving his health, and I submit it should be cleared with me. If the home's position is that the ten cigarettes will be administered daily, I ask that the health authority case manager for Matt's file to start a meeting, ASAP. He is not permitted to smoke over eight cigarettes per day with me and that

will not be changing at any material time. Again, neither he nor I can afford such an increase, and it is not remotely in his physical health interests.

Thank you for your understanding.

    And with that, I am beyond a prelude to a breaking point — I am in so far now, the only way out is to escape.

CIRCULAR ARGUMENTS

S aturday with my son, December 24th! YES! It was all I could muster to not cry when I picked him up from the group home last night. I had missed him so much.

We started our morning with dark roast coffee! Both of us awakened raw-tired... but this mix put us both in the mood we love to share — high energy, ready to tackle the world (for him, away from the group home that has him distressed, and for me — outside and distanced from Hell House, a less than palatial estate filled with depression, anxiety, negativity, and unmitigated melodrama)...

Matt cried himself to sleep last night. Sadly, he witnessed the manipulation and bullying in Hell House (and in case you're wondering, I have never referred to this property with Mattie as "Hell House." That would be inappropriate and irresponsible). But with what he saw and heard last night, he was shocked and appalled.

"Mom, I feel so helpless. I am *really* worried about you; this is *so* not good. I am so sorry you have to deal with this. But you know it won't last forever — and I'm glad you know that. I wish I could do anything to ease your pain, so if there is anything — please tell me and I will do it. Heck, just being here makes *me* depressed, and I only saw this shite for a couple of hours last night. I don't know how you can do it, Mom; you are so strong it amazes me. I am in awe of you."

AHH, my boy — my light. My why.

I kept my vow — to myself and to Dolores. I cooked nothing for Hell House today on my day off.

Sunday DECEMBER 25, 2016 (Christmas Day)
Well, I will start the day with coffee, then resume all the usual caregiving duties.

Now, I have oatmeal raisin cookies ready to go into the oven. My responsibility for the client's family dinner is to prepare everything except the turkey. So, I've done:

1) long beans with mushrooms, almonds & lemon rind
2) yams & sweet potatoes infused with caramel sauce & pecans
3) pasta salad
4) Brussel sprouts in cheese sauce
5) beans in coconut curry sauce

I still haven't gotten past the fact that I've been forced (never *asked*) to work Christmas Day and begrudgingly prepare half their Christmas dinner. But at least during the times Roxanne is reading or napping, I can spend time in my room watching Netflix with my son.

DO NOT tell me to embrace this, to make the most out of an unpleasant situation. I already do that for things over which I have no control, but I hate every single waking moment of being forced to take part in Christmas and to work with no pay (still my $3.44 hour) on this day.

I spent the ENTIRE day cooking for their Christmas Dinner; exhausted & run off my feet; the dog was a pain in the ass today, too — whining, begging for food incessantly. I tripped over her twice and avoided stepping on her around 4 PM and threw out my back. Lovely.

Roxanne chimed in cantankerous as ever, "I told you to get better glasses. You can *see* Sophie is *right there*. This is her home — and you work around her. You need to pay more attention."

I refused to have dinner at the table with them, saying I wanted this to be their family time. Neither Matt nor I wanted to sit in that dining room. Fortunately, Dolores begrudgingly accepted my decision. Dinner was delicious. Gotta find the blessings in what I call 'the pissy mix.'

I was EXHAUSTED. After dinner, Dolores said, as I was washing the dishes and had about half completed, "Dishes will be my treat." Usually, I would offer a polite, "Are you sure?" but this time, I did not. I said a thank you, but inside I was livid. Why should I wash dishes for *their* family dinner?

I went into the living room around 6:30, to see if she wanted me to take care of Roxanne. She told me she would put her to bed later and to just rest — take the rest of the night off. I suppose she had a brief "Christmas cheer" moment, and she again thanked me for taking care of her mother, adding that was the best present I could give them. Or was that a subliminal dig that I did not buy gifts for them? Yeah, I wondered what kind of foreshadowing this was going to turn out to be?

And, of course, with the women of Hell House — *no good deed goes unpunished*. Dolores then brought up the subject of Cody the Bath Girl again. WTF? On Christmas, after you forced me into slave labor and took away my holiday tradition with my son? When my son is sitting patiently in the bedroom watching Netflix by himself right now?

She told me the health authority had asked her if she wanted Roxanne on the list for other homes (e.g., after the Cody problem, which still keeps coming back to be related to or blamed on me? Truly, WTF?). Darlene said she told them no, keep her on the list for Gemstone — but she said, "If Sarah leaves, I'll be ticked, but I'll manage."

Nope, nada, good night, Missy. Not taking *that* guilt bait, either. When I have my money and secure a rental, I will be leaving.

I have been taken advantage of, manipulated, and guilted into working far more than I should have. Now, Dolores is taking this another step too far, trying to guilt me into staying here because caring for her mother is so difficult for *her*. She also tried to tell me I need to see the videos sent from the grandchildren to Roxanne. Though I did not verbalize it, I DO NOT CARE. I have zero interest. I see what she is trying to do, because she keeps saying, "You're one of the family — this is your HOME..."

Not only am I not one of the family, never have been, never will be... With the narratives of Roxanne being on the Gemstone list, with the return comments about Bath Girl and inferring anything in that was my fault, I detest and resent the situation even more, yet I recognize it for precisely what it is. They have found someone with a good work ethic here, and they are milking it. They want to pull me down, trap me and enslave me.

Not today, Chickie. DEFINATELY not today!

DECEMBER 26, 2016

Matt awakened, depressed; he is SO sad about what he has witnessed here. He says he HATES Roxanne — and he has never in his life expressed that about any elderly person. "I am mad at myself for ever calling her Gramma. I thought all seniors were sweet. Guess they're like every other person in the world."

I reminded him there's good, bad, and neutral everywhere.

He is so anxious about me. I am so sorry he has seen the minimal dysfunction that he has, but I also did not want him to be alone over a major holiday — in a home where he is exceedingly uncomfortable and resenting and dreading each next interaction.

He elaborated he has been feeling depressed at the group home, as well. He cries often, but he is afraid to tell them (1) because they could use it against him to push his buttons, and (2) because they could make him take more medication that could mess with the balance he has enjoyed for so long.

Bottom line, he gets no exercise. He did mess up his opportunity to attend the gym with the indoor walking track when he smoked marijuana there. He told me, "Mom, I fucking hate myself for doing that. I am so broken. I really want to do the right thing, but I also want to feel good."

Brain injury exacerbated by impulsivity and addictions. My poor boy.

I promised him his secret is safe with me, and I promised him that once I am out of here, we will exercise together. That will defeat his depression.

I am so worried about what will happen to Mattie when I die. The group home is better than "being on the street," but it needs to be monitored for quality care (cigarettes disbursed, lack of exercise, inappropriate nutrition)...

All this subject came up on arising this morning, with him so worried about me. He asked, "Mom, do you ever think of suicide when you are here? I understand it is *that* bad."

I told him I am a little sad, and I have some stress — but I have him, and seeing him every six days keeps me moving forward. Besides, I would never abandon him — I made that promise even before he was born.

He was happy to hear that, though I don't think he ever doubted it. I have never abandoned him, not even during times when everyone else around me tried to convince me to do so.

I reminded him this is only temporary.

"Yeah, this too shall pass like gas, Mom! First, it hurts, then it stinks — then you forgot all about it when it's gone."

Only going to say this about THAT. We survived yesterday's "holiday" but it was a freak show. I resent being forced to take part in a family's Christmas that had nothing to do with me. I resent being forced to cook and clean for a family's Christmas and to perform work for which I was not hired or even asked to accommodate. I resent the manipulative comments thrown my way, and the continued bullying. I resent that the entire day made my son horrified by what I endured here, made him cry, and made him depressed. He awoke this morning saying, "Mom, I am SO SORRY you have to go through this. I am so worried about you." Then, his usual, "I love you, Mom."

Oh buddy, I sure do love you, too.

Despite a shortfall of $150 every month for my financial obligations, because I am so grossly underpaid here, I again sought to be "the better person." I spent $17 of my meager funds and bought two books for Roxanne's Christmas, one from me and one from Mattie. I spent another $1 on wrapping paper. Despite opening them in front of me and Matt, she never once said thank you. It hurt Mattie *deeply* — he was stunned. He is so attuned to etiquette, and despite his many shortcomings, I have always found myself proud of how polite and respectful he remains.

Mattie wanted to choose the book he would gift to Roxanne. He was careful to take time for thoughtful consideration. When we had shopped for this, he told me, "Mom, I want to get something to make her smile. Dogs always make me smile. And she *has a dog*, so she must *like* dogs." He chose "A Dog's Purpose."

Every dog happens for a reason.
W. BRUCE CAMERON
A
DOG'S
PURPOSE
THE *NEW YORK TIMES* AND
USA TODAY BESTSELLER

NOW A MAJOR MOTION PICTURE

*Mattie's carefully
considered gift to
Roxanne*

With this visit, he lost all respect for Roxanne when he observed her true nature... and again, this is a first in Mattie; he *loves* seniors.

The only thing that will guide me through to the other end of this is (1) two days with my son each week, and (2) knowing that when I can rent my own apartment, I will leave forthwith. This prison has affected my health adversely, and it is physically apparent now.

Here's to survival, and living to fight another day.

DECEMBER 27, 2016

Roxanne was pleasant last night, and we had a very good morning. She seems much more relaxed. I listened when she wanted to chat. She opened up to me about how rough Dolores was on her. I actually thought I saw kindness under her gruff and frail exterior. She has been significantly more kind and *genuine* today. We've had some good chats.

It saddens me every time I hear Dolores forbid her to talk about the olden days, snapping, "Mom, those days are LONG gone."

I feel these remembrances are very important to Roxanne. I encourage her to talk, and she does. This morning Dolores (while here, and after introducing Crystal, today's bath girl) suggested I use the oranges she brought down. This irritated me, but I kept that to myself, as I am managing just fine here and have wasted absolutely nothing. She said, "If you make juice, I will take it up to my place and use it."

REALLY? Make juice for her? What's wrong with her taking those oranges back up to her house and taking care of herself? Inside my head, I was saying to myself, "Make your own friggin' juice." I told her I would make an orange sauce for left-over turkey.

With a slight tone of resentment, she told me, "Yeah, I *guess* you could do that." Indeed, I can and I will. I detest her pushiness... I now see her for the grand manipulator that she is. Recognizing now that the apple doesn't fall far from the tree, I now see her as the miserable and disgruntled woman that she is. I will be her fresh-squeezed orange juice butler.

ANYHOW, the new bath girl is fine. She's amicable enough; and Dolores set her straight right up front — that I AM NOT HERE. THIS IS MY TIME OFF. Roxanne also took up for me (I could overhear the kitchen conversation), saying that Cody was very inappropriate last week. Good on her. Since she instigated all that, why couldn't she be a mature adult and "fess up" sooner? Why all the gaslighting?

This morning, I performed the usual duties, cleaned Roxane's bathroom and mine... swept three porches of snow, made the fire and kept it going, and let the dog out six times (Sophie did not eat her breakfast again; was sick — vomited and had diarrhea on the floor around noon. I cleaned it up, being of a mind that the new bath girl should not have to do that).

I will use leftover turkey and make an orange sauce for it. I will cook the ailing cauliflower that's in the fridge and use the leftover broccoli.

Crystal said a polite, but phony, goodbye on leaving. I assess her personality as doing what she needs to do, but saw the disdain for me in her eyes and her tone. I suppose the health authority must have given her some kind of warning, based on the rhetoric of Cory the Bath Girl. Or, for all I know, perhaps Cody is her friend. WHATever. *Certainly, I will not mention this to anyone; otherwise, I will be perceived as over-reactive and paranoid; but I have now learned to trust my observations and assessments and to keep it as that — an observation and education.*

She left the toilet seat up, she left debris in the sink, she did not leave the cold water dripping onto the sponge as she found it (fortunately I paid attention; we certainly don't want frozen pipes down here), she left red paint on a kitchen cabinet door (from working with paints with Roxanne), and she let the fire go out (WHATever). Next week, if this same bath girl returns, I will make sure I leave for the time she is here.

DECEMBER 28, 2016

It's Wednesday morning, and coffee is a necessity — not a luxury today.

Despite two sleeping pills last night, I had almost no sleep. I had two nightmares — one of me awaiting the electric chair, asking the doctor if I could have a sleeping pill beforehand... On awakening from that one, I looked at the clock at 4 AM and clearly nodded off, as I was awakened by the dog barking in her crate at 4:28. That's early — and was a first. Wonderful (not)...

So now I am up for the day, and it is *not* a good feeling. I am a morning person, but NOT TODAY.

Just when you think it's safe to go back in the water? I have some concerns with a couple of mixed signals from Dolores today.

Last night, she made a comment (when bringing in groceries for the week), "I don't care if you don't have time to get the housework done." WTF? I work VERY hard, do housework EVERY SINGLE DAY, all day long in actuality, and have a schedule I have lived by for five consecutive weeks here. This place has NEVER suffered for cleanliness. I totally do not get where she's coming from, but wanting to avoid any uncomfortable interaction with her, I just ignored her comment and did not "take the bait."

Then, I recalled that when I first arrived here (Day One), Dolores (in the kitchen) told me a story about one caregiver who had left dishes in the drainer to dry... never put them away. Dolores came in and put them away one day, and the caregiver allegedly questioned her on it. Dolores alleges she told her, "YES dishes were to be put away". But on Christmas day, as I was putting dishes away, she said to me, "Drip dry — don't you know about that one?" WTF? I intend to carry on as I WOULD DO IN MY OWN HOME, and that is to keep dishes put away at all times. I dislike clutter & disarray. And it is not lost on me that if I had let dishes "drip dry," I would have been lectured on how to play in the sandbox. Not today, Chickie. Not today.

Dolores has been in a good mood for three days now. We've had good chats. I let her talk about her past/her history, particularly as her daughter sadly discourages it. I believe memories are the most of what a person age 92 can have. She enjoys talking about the past.

Turns out, she also enjoys having Mattie around; she talks about him often. Every time she drinks her cranberry juice and makes her squinty face in disgust, she remembers how Mattie loved it! That was very nice to see/hear. She insisted he stay for my days off and into the Sunday (New Year's Day), and that I just take him back when she went back for her nap. Very nice. I will do that.

Dave has been very sweet, consistently, too. When he was outside chopping and stacking wood this morning, I went out to say hello and thank him. I could tell he appreciated that. I doubt he gets much in the way of appreciation from Dolores. He also said if we got snowed in, either he or Dolores would return Mattie to the group home on Monday. Very nice.

11 AM — and since Dolores randomly suggested housework was not completed (malarky), I itemize:
- I have brought in four buckets of wood (stacked two, have two sitting on the floor)
- I have swept floors
- I have vacuumed
- I have watered plants
- I have provided Roxanne's breakfast
- I have culled the dead flowers from her fresh arrangement gifted by Robert
- I have tried to brush the dog, albeit unsuccessfully, but I did it in front of Roxanne so she could confirm to Dolores the dog needs to see a professional (yeah; I said I wouldn't but I am trying to keep the peace)
- I have let the dog out six times (yes; I track this)

- I have washed dishes, dried them, and put them away
- I have cleaned Roxanne's commode and inserted a fresh bag
- I have restoked the fire (new logs) seven times since 4:30 AM when the dog woke me up
- I have shaken the rugs/vacuumed in the mudroom (grateful for no snow/ice to clear from the porches today)

DECEMBER 29, 2016

Roxanne rang her bell at 7:24 AM... I was in the middle of starting the fire. I let Sophie out first, then attended to her. Sophie barked for re-entry for 15 minutes, but had to wait. I was late getting the fire together, as I needed to give Roxanne her juices & porridge and let the coffee drip (fortunately I had set up the coffee last night, so I only had to press the button).

I changed bed linens; did laundry; finally got the fire going; brought in two more buckets of wood, stacked the remaining wood into a bin outside (which Dolores left lying in the snow). I told Roxanne I did that, but I got no reaction. Since I do not want that to be construed as an integral part of my duties, I will not do it again. I could almost "see the wheels turning" in Roxanne's eyes.

AND, our abbreviated 2nd honeymoon phase with Christmas festivities, seems to have concluded. I got more mixed signals from Dolores last night when she was here around 7:30 (she brought down the mail). She negatively referred to me taking Friday and Saturday off instead of Thursday and Friday, noting I'd changed my mind. I slightly snapped (my boundaries projected, although it was a gentle snap from what I would *like* to put forward) that we'd agreed before that my days off would change contingent with the weather and that those days off revolved around Mattie. She said nothing further.

I recited what I'd done in the day's course and saw no gratitude for it. Rather, her comment was, "You've left nothing for me to do when I'm here." WTF! Isn't that the idea, to leave nothing so she cannot bitch about things she concocts for me to do? She clearly has done that with every other caregiver hired here. I don't want to go there, so I live in paranoia here to avoid it. I told her I would change Roxanne's bed linens tomorrow (Thursday) and she said I could leave that until Friday. NO FUCKING WAY... I told her it's my usual schedule, so I'd keep to that. She could just relax on Friday and Saturday. She said nothing. I get the idea she wants me to leave it, so she can DO it and bitch about it, or *not do it — and criticize me for not doing it on the designated day.*

She gave me a grocery gift card with $35 left on it, in case there were emergency supplies that needed to be bought. I told her I would keep receipts. She said not to, but I'm not buying into *that* speculative distrust when monies are spent, either. I will keep and present receipts, and return the card when it is empty.

I so look forward to seeing Mattie tomorrow.

BUT WAIT — THERE'S *MORE*! Another WTF moment.

A few short weeks ago, both Roxanne *and Dolores* asked why I bother coloring my hair and encouraged me to just let it come in naturally. Now, today, they have *both* commented on how I should color my white roots? WTF... Do they have meetings to plan how they will both simultaneously provoke me?

How is this any of their concern? So, this means that in my absence — some time off, these two women are gossiping conjectures and judgments. I told them both I would not waste my hair color until I had a reason to look presentable for someone. Yeah, that's right — not worth my $15 to color-up for this prison. There's no one here to impress.

7:16 PM now. Roxanne has been mostly pleasant after the hair-color criticisms. But she truly is paranoid around her daughter and about doing anything "against the rules." Heck, I am too — with *both* women. She wanted to talk about Gemstone today and asked me to send her a link so she could read about it online. I did. Then, she panicked and asked me to delete it because she didn't want Dolores to see she'd been reading about it. WTF.

BUT, she returned to her talents of annoyance this evening. "It's time to do my blood work" (this said at 7:05).

"Nope, not until 7:30." "*OH*, yeah," was her disgruntled response. She also bugged me about "my fire" going out, and I told her it was not out, the log was catching and it would go full-on soon. She has returned to castigating me at every turn — having her fun, feeling her power.

I fight to hold back my tears, and I am so tired... and the stupid *dog* has driven me half insane today. Roxanne was resting and the dog wouldn't stop whining. I sent her out, and she galloped back in and to her food bowl and looked up at me (knowing I am *her* servant, too). It is *not* her feeding time. When I ignored her, she whined incessantly. We repeated this six times in 1.5 hours. I have almost tripped over her again several times... I despise the dog now. I don't recall *ever* feeling animosity towards an animal until now and I feel slightly ashamed of that. Like Mattie, I have always loved animals.

I was also annoyed with Roxanne inserting herself into my personal life today, asking if I would rent or buy a place when I moved from here/when my position was done. I told her I had no savings, and I had no job — so I could never buy a place, especially at this age. She insisted *she* did, so I could... I could get a used trailer like she did and fix it up myself. WTF. I did not even dignify that idiocy with commentary. Her sons and Dave helped her with some minor renovations, and the trailer was purchased for $2,500. She uses hydro and water from Dave and Dolores' property, pays no rent for the land use, and does not contribute to property taxes.

I hate this place with a passion. When the time comes for my escape, I will be elated. I desperately need to return to the gym, to combat encroaching depression. I cannot endure much more of this situation.

At 8:05 PM, I gently went to see Roxanne in the kitchen, to take her back to her room (8 PM being the norm). She said she was ready to go to bed, but *purposefully (with undeniable intention)* moved slower than ever, reading more in her book, fumbling with her bookmark, playing with her Kleenex. She even made eye contact with me — this is how I knew it was purposeful. I stood there for ten minutes, and finally said, "We're going back." I removed the brakes from her chair and carted her back; she was a drama queen the entire way.

"Oh, you're hitting every bump on the floor! Ouch! Ouch!" WTF.

In her room, she again took more than her usual time to even try to leave the wheelchair to transfer to the commode. Then, she stood and more slowly than ever put her teeth into the cup of Polident water. Once again, she made eye contact with me and continued her slow-motion movements. Finally, she begrudgingly let me slide down her trousers and sat down. Once seated, I reminded her, "If you wake up early tomorrow, be sure to phone Dolores — as I will not be here."

"OH?" This was uttered as though she was surprised?

"Are you coming back tomorrow night?" I said yes, but it might be late. "Are you bringing Matt?" I replied yes. "OK" was her response. I feel she knows my days are numbered; it's only a matter of time and the time is drawing nigh.

I put her to bed; this is the second night she has failed to wipe herself after defecating. I suppose that is my job now, too? Now, five weeks in, she has only done this over the past two consecutive nights. Is she declining physically and cognitively, or is she purposefully giving me a harder time? I think it is the latter. The strategized bullying seems to show her cognitive abilities are *not* impaired. She's sharp as a tack and as prickly as a rusted one.

DECEMBER 28, 2016

There were significant goals strategized and achieved between 2014 and 2016, but one goal fell very short and by the wayside — that being my joy of life in employment. Despite having altered my course, and moved closer to my son (no regrets about being in Kamloops), I now find myself trapped in the absolute worst working conditions of my life. Instead of seeking *more* job satisfaction, my next move will be toward seeking *any* job satisfaction.

Where employment goals/satisfaction are concerned, I wish to be paid more than $3.44 per hour. Yes, when I calculated the hours I am required to work and to provide on-call availability, and subtract the 1.5 days off in a week, I earn $3.44/hour. YES, my room and board are covered — but I have no ability to personalize my room and I may not choose my meals. I am also told when I can take a shower.

I wish to not be manipulated, ridiculed, and bullied in a passive-aggressive environment... I wish to choose the food I wish to eat. I wish to sleep at night without nightmares, and not cry several times a day... And I wish to see my son visit me and not cry himself to sleep because he witnesses what is transpiring here.

'Nuff said. It is what it is. I made a rash decision to take this position just so I could be closer to my boy... It will not be forever unless I actually die in one of my multiple nightly nightmares. But for now, it is a living hell, and if one more person tells me to embrace the learning, I am going to consider a wide-angled bitch slap. Living in hell is appropriate for a home called "Hell House."

The thing about those "rash decisions" — those spur-of-the-moment necessary responses to crisis — there's no time to effect *rationality* as you're operating from a sense of desperation. A group home or an apartment residence goes sideways, and there is little time to plan, strategize and react. The first thing you do (I DO) is to look around and guestimate what needs to be sold and what must be kept and moved (with a financial cost and a physical expenditure attached to that), the search for right-now-ready accommodations on short notice leaves you with a dredged-bottom set of selections. You choose what you can afford and the lesser of the evils. There is no time to research what neighbors are in the vicinity, much less what kind of property owner with whom you are dealing. It did not differ from accepting the position here at Hell House. I interviewed, they presented well, and I took the job, packed and made the costly and excruciating move across a highway known as BC's Highway to Hell, multiple times, with my brain-injured son in tow.

I face the inevitable reality, too, that when I am able to rent my personal apartment in the city, I will accept dredged-bottom availability. I already presume that my escape route will be another temporary accommodation. For now, *getting out* is the primary goal.

DECEMBER 30, 2016

Well, it's been another exceedingly hard week, filled with manipulation tactics and melodrama... But I survived! And today and tomorrow are my days off. I swear, they've never been so welcomed.

I have hair color on my roots, and I'm about to do my nails. I haven't cared about my appearance since week two here, but I do this for Mattie, so he doesn't worry about me when he sees me less than optimal. Of course, part of me knows I will feel more confident after tending to my grooming again.

I will "coffee-up" soon, although I don't *dare* wake the dog and begin all that incessant, ridiculous whining for food and attention until I'm ready to leave!

I can't stop the waves, but I'm teaching myself to surf!

Another New Year

What a messed-up start to the day. The new year brings hope of positive change, but not THIS year. 2017 arrived on the fog of a storm ever brewing, and no amount of perky smiles and positive demeanor seemed capable of altering that.

Dolores was in a pushy, bitchy mood... trying to tell me how to live my life, to get antibiotics, to eat ice cream for my throat (knowing full well I started my nutrition plan today). She told me she'd be making ham instead of salmon for dinner, and I told her not for me, but thanks. She gave me that "you think you're better than all of us" attitude and look, and I reminded her of my Jewish faith. "That's just stupid," she droned.

Nice. I didn't even bother with the rhetoric of how pigs will eat anything, and they were filthy animals rendering meat with high sodium and fat contents. Heck, we all know from the stories of the Willie Pickton farm horrors in the Lower Mainland that pigs will also consume a human body — make it disappear in short order. Nope, I let that one say inside my head.

She snapped, and I snapped back on a couple of conflicting opinions and breached boundaries. I walked away. I despise her. I am not even going to re-live all the commentaries that spewed from her mouth, but the one that prompted me to walk away and leave her sitting there alone was "You're just silly refusing to eat pork and shellfish just because some old goats in black hats in Israel told you it's bad for you? You're a grown woman — make your own fucking decisions. Smarten up – pork, bacon, ham, sausage — it's all *delicious*... You mean to tell me if you had a lobster tail in front of you, you wouldn't eat it?"

I told her, "No — just like the ham, the pork chops, the prawns — I do not eat pork and shellfish, but I don't deny you from eating it; I will even cook it for you when you want it."

Although Matt was in my room, watching a Netflix movie on the bed with headphones, he did not hear this exchange. Never knowing what will spew from these women's mouths at Hell House, I set up those headphones for him at Christmas, too.

Still, Matthew was so very sad, so very appalled because he witnessed her manipulation and bullying in the course of his visit. I am so sorry he saw any of that; I truly thought Dolores would respect my son and at least wait until he was gone to belittle and degrade me. Instead, her power trip included hurting my son. Mattie has implored me to leave without notice as soon as I can rent a place in the city. I had wanted to persevere, but my mind *was* leaning toward shielding my mental health. I need to be of positive thinking to guide Matthew through the tumultuous decline in his group home.

I have never been one to vacate any employment without notice, but case in point, if an assisted living facility calls or if Roxanne dies, I would be afforded no notice. It was Matt that reminded me of this. "Mom, why would you worry about giving notice when they would never give YOU that respect? Why would you do anything for people that are so intent (is that the right word, Mom?) on seeing you trapped? It's not like Gramma will suffer — her mean daughter will suffer and I think she deserves that. You're always telling me we all have consequences for our actions, so she does, too." Despite his deficits and shortcomings, he exhibits great insights and wisdom frequently now.

He continued, "That woman has been *such* a disgruntled bitch and I am really sick of her snide comments, her know-it-all attitude, and her treating you like you are her slave and like you are stupid — like you are a loser. I hope you show her you are better than this by leaving."

He actually used the word "disgruntled". Wow. Blessings in the pissy mix.

Given the extremely low wage paid in this position, I can only hope to strategize vacating within the next eight weeks. By the time my backlogged monies owed arrive (which should happen end of January), I should be owed about $2,500. That will be sufficient for my exit.

January 1st has been traditionally one of our favorite holidays, with putting pen to paper and mind to mouth for a list of what we could do to improve our lives, on small levels and with larger goals in the plan. We usually start a new Gratitude Jar, which we fill with notes of blessings, wonderful days, and great successes, and typically read on New Year's Eve at the end of the year.

Today was not one of those days, met with conflict and animosity and belittling at every turn. I am so sorry Matt had to witness the conditions in this household, but he wanted to be with me. And he did not want to be in the group home on New Year's Day.

And guess what Dolores brought in the next bag of groceries from her freezer? Frozen ham, pork chops, bacon, and lobster tails. 'Ya really can't make this stuff up!

LIVING AND DYING AT HELL HOUSE

I t's the second day of a brand new year. January 2, 2017.

I adamantly believe all of us are held accountable for how we react to unpleasant situations... *Sure*, we all have unforeseen drama & trauma hit us broadside, through no fault of our own. Beyond owning up to anything we might have done to bring the unfortunate circumstances to our forefront and ensuring we never make that same inadvertent response or action again, we simply have to find the lesson, carry on, fight like a warrior and come out the other end, better for having suffered.

The living environment I am trapped in is both abnormal and unhealthy. It actually feels *unsafe*. I suffer emotional abuse and bullying every single day; I remain silent for that which is unworthy of response and extend firm, yet professionally polite (though readily accepted as "fair warning"), boundaries when just too much is slammed my way.

There's a bizarre and morbid approach to living and dying here at Hell House. The daughter *and* my client (e.g., not hearsay) related the story of how her brother passed in this same trailer less than a year ago... shortly after the fall Roxanne took (which resulted in her permanent wheelchair confinement), her son (obese at 370 lbs) lived here as her caregiver. She rang her bell from the bedroom one day and he said out loud, "Coming." He fell (the client heard him crash), and said, "Oh my, I've fallen too." Abrupt silence followed.

Those were his last words... Several minutes passed, and the client phoned the daughter (who lives 50 meters up the hill on the same property). She said the son had fallen and hadn't said another word. The daughter said she would be there in a few minutes, adding that she was busy! She arrived 15 minutes later, found him face-down on the kitchen floor, and called an ambulance. They advised her to turn him over and begin CPR. In her own words to me, she said, "He's almost 400 lbs, I was not even *trying* to flip him over. I told them to 'Just send an ambulance.'"

They apparently pled with her to start CPR and she adamantly refused. She is a Registered Nurse, to boot. They arrived 30 minutes later to a DOA response. The daughter had no remorse; she laughed as she told the story to me, this day. I can hardly believe what exists in this household.

I have also been instructed NOT to initiate CPR if Roxanne suffers a heart attack or stroke. I said I needed to see an originally signed "DNR." None was ever produced, but while organizing the client's telephone directory recently, I found one. I scanned it and kept a copy for myself, and posted the original under a magnet on the fridge. The daughter's exact words to me were, "Let the old lady die — she's lived long enough. We've all had enough of this shit."

Another conversation ensued over the elderly dog here — that if she gets to be any more trouble (whining, seeking attention) they will just put her down. I have problems with that, too... I don't *like* the dog — but she does not deserve to be exterminated simply because she is inconvenient. She has been in the family home with Roxanne for almost two decades.

The client is 92. My grandfather lived within a couple of days before turning 106 and enjoyed excellent mental acuity and health until age 105 when his Alzheimer's onset began and he could no longer safely live independently. I remembered something my mother had said, so many years ago — that "The old man was here long enough." And I wonder — not having close family relationships other than with my son — is this normal? Do others speak the same way? I know, 100 percent, I would *never* revel in my son's passing — not as long as he was healthy and devoid of pain, and even then, I would not *revel*; I would be tormented, heartbroken and in despair to lose my son. In fact, cannot imagine life without him, though one day — it is likely he will have to face life without me.

I came here intending to make someone's life better, more comfortable, and pleasant in their elder years. That, sadly and unfortunately, was NOT their purpose in securing someone for this position. Also clear are the reasons no caregiver has stayed more than a few weeks (I was told that one lasted six months, then told, in actuality, it was 16 weeks)... ALL have left with no notice. I also understand that.

The only focus that keeps me moving forward is (1) my son and (2) knowing this will not last forever. There will be a light at the end of the tunnel in about eight weeks. I must remain stable, hold my boundaries in place, and my head high, until that time.

Mattie cries every time he comes here because he is so sad and appalled... but he also admires my strength and it's a good example to set for him — plus he appreciates his group home a bit more than he did. "Mom, I feel things are not great at my group home — but what you live with here is *so much worse.*"

I've been sick for a while, but my throat is now slightly better — though still bleeding and still swollen. I had a shower and felt better with that, too...

AND we begin another day. It's 6:50 AM, and time to ready myself for "commencement ceremonies" at 7 AM (dog out, juices & porridge out, a fire started). I got Roxanne up at 8:10; she was still sleeping. Another grumpy mood starts the day. Great.

She was a drama queen on the transfer down the hall. Great. I just ignored it all; her breakfast, coffee, juices & meds were on the table. Sophie had been fed and relieved herself outside twice, and the fire was blazing.

I put on my coat and a toque, and despite still being sick, I ventured outside and brought in another bucket of wood; stacked it inside. I cleaned the tiles and shook out the throw rugs. Today, we are at minus 27 degrees. Then, I proceeded into the kitchen to do my personal meal prep for four days (used the leftover turkey breast for protein, since Roxanne had told me, "I don't want any of that dry shit; just throw that out"). I made rice pudding for Roxanne, as it is one of her favorites.

Dolores trampled in (no good morning), slamming down more wood in the living room; she tracked in all kinds of debris and never cleaned up after herself. She also tracked debris down the hallway, over my impeccably clean floors.

She also used Roxanne's toilet and left the toilet seat up with her gigantic defecation in the bowl unflushed. Yesterday she left urine in the toilet and did not flush, and per her usual, poured it in without lifting the seat. I always have to clean up dried urine on the toilet seat. I am confident she does this intentionally since I am the slave labor and she enjoys displaying her power. She also left dirty countertops in the kitchen and filthy debris all over the floors.

> Power trip — defined as "something that a person does for the pleasure of using power to control other people."

She finally came inside, and to her credit (for which I said thanks, twice) she brought me more 222s. She asked how I was feeling; I said, "Still sick, but no fever, though I can barely swallow." I added I tried her ice cream advice last night, and it made things much worse.

She suggested I use a heat pack on my throat; I said I didn't know about that; then she said, "Use an ice pack." This woman regurgitates crap out of her mouth randomly at every turn. I despise her, and I am ashamed of myself for allowing myself such useless emotion.

She bent down in the hallway to pick up a feather (from a pillow) and said, "This is twice I've picked a feather up off the floor." WTF?

I told her I had already cleaned the floors this morning and would not clean them again until tomorrow morning now.

Roxanne was a bitch when I transferred her back at 11:30 to pee. She had wet her underwear again. I always check to see if her trousers are wet, and if not, I put the same ones back on her. She snarled demandingly at me, "Are those wet?" She was watching everything I did.

I snapped, "I've been doing this for seven weeks and I have *never* put wet trousers back on you." She said no more.

When I wheeled her back down the hallway, at a careful, slow speed, she was the drama queen again, whining, "Ouch!" over every bump. My pity and empathy platforms have expired now.

I count the hours — not the days — to my escape.

PERFORMING LIKE A CIRCUS CLOWN

R oxanne has fallen into a habit of asking me to "perform" on protocol items
   before they're due. Can I have my lunch (at 11:15, when the protocol timing
for that is 12 noon)? So now, I always have it prepared at 11:30 and out for her.

Today, after doing that, I was dishing her out some rice pudding in the kitchen
when she whined (her celery not yet finished), "Can I have some pudding?"
I snapped (I've truly had enough of this balderdash), "I am dishing out your
pudding *right now*. You know I *always* give you dessert."

"There have been many things that have been unhealthy for me here, but I am
responding by eating healthy and exercising again."

Again, she looked like she wanted to argue, but she stopped herself.

"Hmph," she grunted sarcastically in her all-knowing rendition, "You will ever
stop sweets, 'cause you *love 'em*. You can't fool me. I've been around the block more
times than you have."

"Yes, I enjoy them, but I won't eat them because they will kill me. I recently went
a full year with zero sugar." I reminded her that until recently, I was a competitive
bodybuilder. What I do, how I eat, and how I live my life — requires structure
and discipline. I also enjoy setting those examples for Mattie, because he cannot
survive without structure and discipline.

She shook her head and rolled her eyes like I had spoken obscenities, adding
judgementally, "I don't know why you would want to do that to your body; you
looked *so bad* — you were pretty and made yourself ugly. You don't make sense."

I detest Hell House and all it represents — with every passing moment. It's no
wonder her husband left her long ago, and it's understandable that no caregivers
lasted more than a few days.

JANUARY 3, 2017

Ashley was the bath girl today; very sweet and bubbly. She did a good job, save and except for putting a wet log on the fire — which extinguished the flame. But hey — unlike the others who all refused to touch that fire and *tried* to let it extinguish, she tried. She deserves credit for that! She's like I was when I first arrived here — no experience with country living and wood-burning stoves.

She also left the washer door open (it's a front-loader and that's a narrow hallway in there), and the toilet seat up – but everything else was excellent – so GREAT job. I can remedy all that easily enough — and if I do *not*, there will be hell for me to pay with Dolores.

I left as soon as she arrived and returned at 1:15, and quietly entered my room (said hi to Ashley who was putting a load in the washer when I arrived). I did not say hello to Roxanne – after all, this is MY time – and I am not family).

I made meatloaf, mac & cheese & prepped sautéd mushrooms & onions, and will add some frozen mixed veggies for tonight's dinner. I will send some meatloaf to Dolores & Dave, but typically she refuses. WHATever. If Dave is there at the door, he will be thrilled to have it.

Dolores pissed me off again today (what else is new?)... I brought out the red ski jacket and asked if Cheryl (a very kind bath girl from the health authority) attended, could she give her the coat and tell her it was from me?

She said "Sure", but tried to put it on herself. Dolores is a size 24; the jacket is a 12 — but a very expensive, good-quality coat — good to 50 below.

I was going to keep it for myself and use it when I diet down this next time, but Cheryl needs a good winter coat right now, and I wanted her to have it.

"Don't even go there with me – you will never fit into this coat, any more than I will."

Countdown to escape; the wench has no idea who or what I am, what I have overcome and accomplished.

Oh, how I detest this waste of human flesh.

I had a lovely visit with Mattie. We went for coffee and a Timmy's breakfast croissant, and drove to find an apartment complex called "Arcadia Towers". It's a nicely appointed building in a wonderful location, but their waitlist is two years, I was told. Plus, a studio suite is $1,250. Out of my league, until I secure genuine work in legal again.

I have another advert, but only the telephone number — no address, so tomorrow when Roxanne cannot hear me and there's no risk of Dolores
being here.

I also mentioned to Dolores I'd like to take Friday-Saturday as days off this week and she said that would be fine, since a friend of Dave's is in town Thursday. Whatever. I have no intention of letting her renege on her word that I can have any days off except Tuesday.

Next week, I will resume with Thursday and Friday as my days off. I'm not assuming the position anymore — heck, I'm not even continuing in the position soon!

I woke Roxanne from her deep sleep napping at 5 PM. She was falling asleep at the table after I wheeled her in for dinner. I had to wake her up and remind her to eat her meatloaf. Begrudgingly, she ate half of a very small portion.

She told me she wanted to go to bed at 6:10 when I woke her up at the table. I warned her Dolores would be back with groceries, and she didn't wanna get caught sleeping. But I also offered to call Dolores on her cell phone, to ask if that was okay — and Roxanne *shrieked*, "Don't you dare! I'll just sit here and sleep. Leave me the fuck alone."

She asked twice what juice was in her glass. "Cranberry juice – same as you get every night."

Dolores ALWAYS has a smart-ass comment. I often wonder if she rehearses these, or practices them in front of a mirror. The first thing out of her mouth when she walked through the door with groceries tonight was, "OH, you cooked fish." NOW, she wants to make me feel uncomfortable because I'll be eating a lot of fish or is she complaining of the aroma of baked salmon? She was the one that bought it. She was the one that questioned me two weeks earlier, "Why aren't you cooking the fish in the freezer? That's good for Gramma."

And still more... I've tried SO HARD to be positive, mentioned to Dolores that Ashley, today's bath girl, was pleasant, and Dolores said negatively, "I still had to take her aside and set her straight, even though she's been here many times, so there was no more kerfuffle."

WTF? She KEEPS implying I had ANYTHING WHATSOEVER to do with Cody's idiocy.

Then, "So you're definitely taking Friday and Saturday off?"

"Yes."

"Good, because I have plans for Thursday."

Do I look like someone who cares?

At 6:30, Roxanne said, "I haven't had my blood work."

"It's not 7:30, Roxanne — you don't get your bloodwork for another hour. Dolores has set 7:30 as the time to check that."

"I know, but I thought you might give me a break for a change."

Devil's advocate — not in my job description.

I am not one to fantasize; I am a reality-check person, through and through — but I keep finding myself joyful at the premise of leaving Hell House with no notice. In fact, that little venture outside of reality is one of the few things that keeps me somewhat sane.

Since Roxanne was sleeping since she finished her dinner, at 7:54 I asked if she wanted to go back a couple of minutes early.

"Yes," and then, "You wanna put a couple of logs on the fire?"

I add a freaking log to that stove every 20 minutes, all day long; PLUS, why in the name of sanity would I want more logs on that fire when I sweat every night, sleep with a fan on me and feel my skin drying so much it's concerning? I told her, "NO, you're going to bed."

She retorts, "Well, I'm going SOMEwhere, don't know if it's to bed."

What in the heck does that mean?

She rocked in her wheelchair for seven solid minutes. A couple of times, she turned her head around and made eye contact with me. I don't know if she was just pushing me, or if she really could not get it together to get out of the chair. Either way, this is not good. She finally asked me to pull her up by the waist of her trousers.

I said, "Well THAT's something new," and I complied.

She sat down on the commode and fiddled with toilet paper and I left her to her privacy while I put her blanket into the dryer and warmed two beanbags, three minutes each. I noticed she had not taken her meds; I took them back to her, along with her cup of water.

I told her she needed to take her meds, and she said, "Oh shit, did I drink my juice?" She would be reprimanded sternly by Dolores for not drinking her cranberry juice.

I told her she did. She watched me insert the bean bags to the base of her bed.

When I got her into bed, she asked if I had her bean bags there.

"YES, and in eight weeks, I have never forgotten them once."

She whined, "My feet are cold."

"Roxanne, you have on three pairs of socks, a warmed blanket wrapped around you like you're a burrito, and two heated beanbags at your feet. I'm not sure what else I can do for you. But I will turn up your heater." I increased the controls from two to four. The max was six.

She asked me to move the heater closer to the bed, and I refused — citing a risk of fire hazards.

Before I could return her water bottle to her tray on the bed (as if we don't remove it when she enters the bed, she invariably knocks it

over), she commanded, "I need my water and I need my book."

Counting the minutes to my escape fantasy, I put the water bottle on her bed and moved her book 12 inches to her chest. I told her I would be back at 9 to turn out the light. I left the room.

I believe I am not healing readily because I am so stressed. I honestly don't know how much more of this I can withstand... but, at the same time,

I have no choice. When we make a choice, we also choose the consequences. I am here, and for now, I am trapped. But that is only temporary.

Again, I count minutes until I can see money magically deposited in my account by the CRA, so I can leave without notice.

Today was another day of Roxanne *trying* to be better in the morning, but invariably returning to treating me as a slave. Dolores had the same demeanor, just a little more passive-aggressive. But hey — I believe in finding the blessing in the pissy mix — and these are GREAT portrayals of what I never want to be in my life. I feel myself becoming bitter and mean in this environment. Even when I was bullied in Kelowna and in Surrey law firms, I never became embittered or cruel, nor did I ever, until now, feel I could become vindictive. Instead, in the past, I felt the pain of it all and walked away. But now, I am less inclined to keep walking away.

After all that hard work I did from 2014 through 2016 to get my health back under control (and thriving), my health is declining again. I have stopped smiling, other than when I am with Mattie, and I have a headache more of the day than not.

But wait! There's more!

8:40 PM

Roxanne has been tucked into bed for 15 minutes. I dressed for bed and just took my sleeping pill.

She rings her bell three times, then shouts, "Did I ring that more than once?"

I get up, turn on my light, walk to her door and ask, "Yes, what can I do for you?"

"I want to get up."

"WHY do you want to get up, Roxanne?"

"Is it too early to get up?"

"It is night, Roxanne. You have been in bed for 15 minutes. It's not time to get up, it's time to sleep."

"OK. I want to go to bed."

I tell her she needs to remove her hearing aid, and the games begin again.

"YOU remove it."

"NO, Roxanne — YOU remove it."

She does so, without issue. I also remind her she needs to remove her teeth; she puts them in the cup (I had the cup there for her at 8 PM but she did not remove her teeth as she normally does). *I refuse to remove that hearing aid; once I do that, she will expect me to do it every night...I will not be further reduced by more "slave tactics." She needs to do that for herself, rather than creating more codependence. I also will never remove her teeth. She is perfectly capable of that, but she has asked me to do that, frequently, as well. I somehow speculated she was planning to bite me, so I declined. It is enough that I am purposefully urinated on at least twice a day and have to wipe her backside when she defecates, because recently she has refused to do so.*

I confirmed she wanted me to turn out the light, and she snapped, "NO!"

I believe she is declining. There is absolutely NO REASON WHATSOEVER for her to be this exhausted.

WHAT A NIGHTMARE. I feel like I'm living in the twilight zone., without the benefit of Rod Serling's narrative guide.

SUSPICIONS OF DEMENTIA

H orrible sleep, despite taking three of those cursed codeine-laden 222s plus two sleeping pills. I am approaching my day with horrific dread, after the turn of yesterday's events. I absolutely must speak with Dolores about this, and I equally dread *that* interaction.

Dolores spoke at great length with Roxanne late morning; after that, Roxanne was better – we seemed to have some great chats... I put her back to read and nap at 2 PM. When I got her up at 5:05, she was indignant once again. No thank you for anything.

At least, she's consistent.

She became progressively worse.... complaining about being cold (despite it being 96 degrees Fahrenheit in the house). I gave her a blanket, freshly warmed in the dryer — no thank you. I gave her dinner (Dolores's chili, brown rice, parsley salad & fresh-cooked carrots). She did not touch the carrots. No one has ever told me Roxanne does not like carrots, yet I have seen her eat them many times before.

Later in the evening, Dolores told me her mother does not like carrots. Then why does she buy them? These women of Hell House thrive on manipulating people with their complaints, baiting, and button-pushing.

She ate nothing at first; I cajoled her – warned her Dolores was coming down. She picked and I provided tea, with no thanks forthcoming, of course. I gave her the dessert (1 tablespoon of rice pudding), and received no gratitude for that, either.

ENOUGH. She picked at her plate again. I told her I'd give her canned soup tomorrow. I said that because when I first arrived here, one complaint about a former residential caregiver was that she could not cook — she only prepared and served canned soups.

She noisily pushed her plate over for me to take away. I did. I threw the food in the garbage.

When Dolores arrived, she lied and said everything was fine. Dolores saw my face and immediately knew otherwise.

"My hip is hurting; could you put some Voltaren on that?"

"Of course." Then, while bending to apply the cream, she purposefully pushed out a fart in my face. Lovely. This is so much fun.

"How'd 'ya like that one? And yes, I know what I'm doing and I'll deny it till the cows come home if you tell on me."

Nope, this is not a case of dementia.

I truly hope G-D takes me home before I ever become this time of human.

JANUARY 4, 2017

Tonight I reached my breaking point; seldom have I come to such a place in my 62 years. I have not yet snapped, but I must admit, I am not quite sure how much more I can endure.

This is *the* most toxic, bizarre environment I have ever observed — and I've seen my more-than-fair share. I believe I actually *did* see evidence of dementia in the client today. This is a ride I am not willing to try.

Holy crap.

JANUARY 5, 2017

Dolores came to get Roxanne up and remind her again to straighten up. Then, she left around 9:15 to take care of her errands in the city; said she would be back after dinner.

At 10:30 AM, I asked Roxanne if she wanted to go back to use the commode, and she had chewed up SOMETHING and regurgitated it into her afternoon meds, and was taking them! I told her, "No, these are for lunchtime."

"Fuck that! They're my meds and I can take them any time between now and lunchtime."

"Really nice, Roxanne. Lovely. Well, you take that up with Dolores — I have my instructions and we're not changing anything in the protocol until Dolores says so. Do you want me to give her a call on her cell, to confirm it's okay for you to have your meds at 10:30 AM?"

I took the remaining meds away from her and set them out of her reach. Enter Bizarro World on another level. Looking at the cheese puffs on her table and the vomited concoction in her meds dish, I realize what she did now. Wow! What's next?

10:45 AM — Sophie puked on the carpet. I told Roxanne (while she was still sitting on the commode), that I would be back, as I had to clean up Sophie's vomit. I made Sophie go outside; she did not want to go. She had still not touched her breakfast.

I resent having to clean up dog vomit.

Dolores asked if we needed anything from the Overwaitea grocery store. I mentioned the dried cranberries and the canned dog food again & she said nothing. She asks but ignores requests, and brings home what she wants. I mentioned that I would be picking up another carton of my almond-coconut milk and the ice cream I want – and she said, "That's your personal items." In other words, it is reaffirmed AGAIN that my groceries are included, but I do not get to choose the kind of milk I have in my coffee... the ice cream I can have, etc. I also resent having to buy a hand crème – since I have never needed it in my life until I came here, hands in chemicals and water, hands in the woodstove). I have asked for latex gloves three times, and each time was told, "Don't be such a pussy; just put your hands in there. You're no hand model."

THANK G-D I can exit in about two months.

At 12:05, I walked past Roxanne to make sure all was good. She whines, "Can I get my pills?"

I reminded her, per Dolores' instructions, "You get your pills with pudding; you don't get your pudding until you finish your vegetables – Dolores' orders."

She only gave me a dirty look. I am confident she knows better than to dispute it. I walked away.

Despite ALL of yesterday's lectures, warnings, etc. from Dolores – all of which were repeated by her again this morning, Roxanne continues to push buttons and try to manipulate.

At 12:30, I walk past to make sure Roxanne is in order; she has scissors, and is picking at the scar on her hand. I ask, "What are you doing with the scissors on your scar?"

She snaps, "I'm *rubbing* it."

"No you're not; I saw what you're doing. Do I need to start taking pictures?"

She put the scissors back and her head down.

She had still not taken her meds. I reminded her she had tried to take them since 10:30 this morning, and that she needs to take them now. Now is the time. I got the nasty and challenging look again, but she slowly fiddled with the dish and began to take them with her pudding.

Roxanne asked to go back to bed at 1:30; I took her. She had a large poop and wiped her own backside without prompting. She knows what is normal, and what is power tripping.

But, when she was entering her bed, she expected me to do the lift and shove. I refused. She asked if I hurt my back yesterday, and I said no – but I told Dolores EVERYTHING that had been asked of me for eight weeks, and Dolores said no to many things, and pushing you in the bed was one.

"Oh, well it'll just take me longer to move over." And with that, she laid there and refused to budge.

"Whatever!" and stood there as she feigned struggle, but got mad enough that she shoved herself over with no problem. "Roxanne, I've given you a *lot* of extras, done a *lot* of things not part of my job description — but all that ends now."

She replied, "Okay."

The more I stay firm and strong-voiced with her, the better response I get. The minute I soften up and become kinder, she changes her tone and walks all over me. Lesson learned.

It's a morbidly interesting lesson revisited. I thought things only happened that way with women bullying in law firms; I saw the same effect in Kelowna, and then again in the Surrey firm... and I've seen it with women in bodybuilding. I do not understand the rationale, but it exists.

I got an email from the group home manager, telling me Matt has had nightmares (allegedly) for a couple of nights, and in the middle of the night, he has been threatening staff, demanding a cigarette.

If there are problems creeping up again, I absolutely cannot handle that, coupled with my trapped situation here. And I cannot disclose that there are *any* issues here in my location.

5:40 PM

At least Roxanne finished her entire dinner (pork chop, asparagus, & oven-roasted potatoes). I congratulated her on it. And just like clockwork, it only took two minutes for her to be critical again, after first complaining about being cold (97 degrees still in the house)."Your fire's burning awfully fast."

So are you cold or not? Do you want the fire extinguished, or do you want it burning and heating your so-called "cold home"?

Case in point, it is so hot in this trailer that each night, I close my bedroom door to sleep — and open my window behind my bed by six inches. Not that I care, but every Bath Girl who has attended here has complained about the excess heating. Certainly, I understand and empathize with Roxanne's frailty – and the fact she always feels cold.

JANUARY 5, 2017

Important reminder — and sad that it's so necessary these days...

I can honestly say that my son has neither been rude nor disrespectful nor has he shunned me for one moment for six and a half years now... Fifteen years of traumatic brain injury, and we're both grateful he has almost zero memory of the first five years. In fact, the last time he did was January 29, 2011.

Yes, I have to document everything. But because I do, you can read this story. If not for comprehensive journaling and retention of correspondence, medical records, and photographs, I would have lost 100 percent of these memories.

BOUNDARIES

O ne week into the new year. Today is January 7, 2017.

Roxanne never said good morning, so I followed suit. She never said thank you for the hearing aid presentation, the warm washcloth, or her brushed dentures. Whatever. Despite being extra careful with her foot when applying her slippers, I got the loud and dramatic "Ouch!" response again. I ignored it and made no eye contact.

When putting a patch of zinc oxide in place for "her crack", as Dolores so eloquently called it, I got *another* loud and dramatic, "Ouch!" Whatever; I ignored that one, too.

"Could you please disengage your wheelchair brakes?"

"*You* do it."

"Roxanne, once again, we are not changing protocols here. At least five times a day, over many weeks, you disengage your own wheelchair brakes."

She snap–bargained, "I'll do it when you give me my shawl."

This time, I used my 'sweet voice,' "I'll give you your shawl once you are seated at the table for breakfast in the kitchen. It's already in there waiting for you."

FINALLY, after I vacuumed, cleared her brekkie and juice dishes, and refreshed her coffee, she tried mustering a kinder approach and asked me to read one of her jokes from her emails. I did. We shared a small chuckle, and I walked away. I prepared her lunch and labeled it for the bath girl, and told Roxanne all I had done (cleaned bathrooms, done laundry, vacuumed, cleaned the back ramp of snow, prepped her lunch, made the fire, etc.). After refreshing her coffee again, I took my shower. First, however, I told her I was taking a shower and asked if she was okay alone for five minutes, to which she meekly replied yes.

When I returned with my hair dried and dressed in clean clothing, I sat down beside her to remind her I was away for four hours today, and then off tomorrow and Thursday — and pointed to the calendar and those days marked off. Reminded her I would not be returning to the house on Wednesday night – but I would be back before dark on Thursday, and would see her on Friday. I talked about making her an angel food cake on Friday with some berries.

"I'd like that," she mumbled.

DONE. Time to leave in 20 minutes and my car is fully loaded. YAHOO! Then I pick up my Mattie after dropping those items at the apartment! My *secret apartment*, about which the residents of Hell House know nothing.

Bath Girl today did not replace the bag in the urine can *and* spilled urine all over my clean floor; she also did not flush the toilet. Because I did not want to be blamed for that, and because a well-paid care aide from the health authority ought to be monitored, I told Dolores and she did not seem concerned with it. Had that been *me*, she would have ostracized me for days. I truly don't get it.

I'm just the house slave, cleaning up other people's messes. Also, Bath Girl folded nothing from the dryer — just left it in a clump on top of the dryer.

When Dolores returned (7:30 PM) with groceries, suddenly Roxanne became hypercritical in her presence.

"The fire's going out!"

I give my head a shake around here so much I may need treatment for whiplash. The fire was not going out, and in any event, Roxanne goes to bed at 8 PM. It is also five degrees above zero outside. She also commanded, "Don't put prunes in my porridge anymore."

Say again? It was Dolores who instructed me to add prunes to her porridge, because she had been constipated for three days. Once again — but at least we're consistent here — no good deed goes unpunished.

Dolores came to me in the kitchen, making excuses for the shit-show of last night, excusing Roxanne's behavior as "just a mistake." She actually called it a "shit show," but it was unusual and nice to appear to be an apology — but I didn't buy into hope for change. After all, I've seen these two at a concert of maladies together.

I told Dolores that the fact remains she was extremely rude — and the crotch shot? Both are unacceptable.

Dolores didn't like my retort but stopped herself from saying anything other than "Well..." and walked away.

Good demon. Walk away. I so look forward to quitting without notice.

Dolores asked, with her challenging tone (yep, I knew it was right around the corner), "Did you have any trouble getting out of the driveway this morning?"

I told her there wasn't a problem when it was five degrees above zero and no new snow. She said nothing, so then I asked her if she saw the text I sent her last night, about me saving Dave some work on shoveling the snow last night — and using the board? She laughed and said she didn't look at her phone. LAUGHED? I suspect she saw me struggle with exiting the driveway last time, likely enjoying the view from her crow's nest seat up the hill. I am her entertainment and at the whim of her discourtesy.

She curtly added, "Well, there's a shovel out there now."

"Yeah, I won't be shoveling any snow here. I still have an email from you when I took this position that in winter, the driveway would be cleared for ingress and egress."

"Well, there's a shovel there, now," she repeated.

There was no gratitude for shoveling the snow for Dave. It is the last time I extend *that* courtesy. She can twist a hip for all I care now. Dave doesn't use that ramp anyway — he merely clears snow from it for *her* safety. These people ask for more and more and more. I am reduced to feeling cruel and almost inhuman, myself. Enough is enough.

Thankfully, the demon waddled home.

When Dolores left, I snapped at Roxanne and told her, "The fire is NOT out — it is just not *blazing*."

She whimpered (now all pretense and meekness), "I thought it was going out."

I snapped, "If you're going to be hypercritical, find someone else do to this!" She looked at me astounded — but remained silent. She knew she had put on a power display for Dolores, but this was the first time I stood my ground so soundly. My intolerance would not be mistaken.

I absolutely cannot last until the end of March. It's an absolute impossibility. I need to vacate by the end of February, so now it's time to re-evaluate that budget again. This is decided.

I have changed, and I don't like what I see in myself. Murphy's Law stands for truth and I expect the worst from everyone. I see things declining with Matthew's group home management and I also expect the worse from that individual, because (like here, at Hell House) Murphys' Law is engaged over there, as well.

So, for now, the goal is to hold boundaries firm here at Hell House, vacate at the first opportunity — and *pray* that things turn around with this new, unlikeable manager at the group home.

ADVOCATING AGAIN

It's time for active advocacy for my son, again. The following was my email to the group home, copied to the health authority.

Dear __:
I haven't heard a response from anyone regarding the request of a few months back to replace his lost BC ID card (it was one year ago today that he finally *got* his BC ID, according to my records, and his expired Access2 Entertainment card — which he has not had since May 31, 2016)... Could you please let me know the status of these two items? Matt should have sufficient funds in his account there to cover both.

ACCESS 2 ENTERTAINMENT
I have provided the online link for your convenience at the conclusion of this email message.

Matt has his expired card; the # on the back of that card is xxx. The cost is $20, and the card is good for five years. He has always carried this card in his wallet and has never lost it. It is my suggestion he continues to carry this in his wallet, to be allowed to be (and feel) responsible for his own ID.

When the BC ID is obtained, it is my suggestion, too, that he is permitted to carry that in his wallet. He has lost no identification carried long term. He is conditioned to putting that back in his wallet in the same place after any use.

The only time in his history of brain injury that ID has gone missing is when he has turned it back into staff... Please note, I am NOT blaming staff, but it should be considered that people get busy, distracted, don't immediately put the

ID in the file where it should go (because they can't) — and mistakes happen; it is just the nature of a busy caregiving practice. I see Matt is becoming more responsible and more careful; I believe he will continue to do so, so long as he has no intermittent or unforeseen stressors in his path. He deserves this responsibility. He will be responsible for the cost of replacing it should he lose it in the future. If he is entrusted with the card(s), only he can be blamed for the loss... When staff is involved in the retention of the cards, then it is frustrating to think he must pay for the loss when it is not necessarily through any fault of his own.

I mean no disrespect with this; rather, I only mean it as it is written.

Thanks again. I look forward to hearing from you.

PUSH AND PUSH BACK

Today is January 8, 2017. I was up this morning at 6, had my shower; went into the laundry room, and saw that Dolores had folded clothes she washed (on *her* duty) but left them for me to put away. Fine; that's what a servant does.

I also noted that she had left no egg cartons to use as a fire starter; whatever — we'll just run out of paper towels early. I refuse to beg and I refuse to remind — as I have learned that is only to be met with criticism, complaint, and more bullying. There's been no kindling for a while, as I refuse to chop wood with an ax. So, no egg cartons and no newspaper or magazines, means the paper towel supply from Costco will make an excellent firestarter.

We teach people how we want to be treated.

And, once again, she did not secure the lid on the jar of cranberry juice, so when I shook it, as with yesterday, cranberry juice went *everywhere* and I had to clean it up. Could this be intentional? I find it hard to believe she does not know what she is doing... although I know she does not want to be providing care for her mother. I also know that if I had left that lid loose, and she spewed it all over the kitchen because of my lack of attention to detail, I would be reprimanded and called an imbecile for days.

One would think she would not push my buttons, saying as she did recently when I refused to shovel snow, groom the dog and chop wood, "Maybe you'll want to find something else." AHHH, but she believes me to be trapped, so she thinks she can mentally torture me and I will simply endure and continue a work ethic out of feeling manipulated and threatened. My, how she doesn't know me! My "being the better person" has led her to believe I will tolerate anything — I will put up, shut up, and perform. If I had a genie in a bottle, oh how quickly I would pack and leave. But alas, I am in a genie-free zone. It's a classic case of kindness mistaken for weakness.

I will assuredly have the last laugh with this nonsense, however. All is in strategic planning now. I will continue on *if* things level out and go respectfully and smoothly; if not, I will take accept my payroll envelopes, remove my effects, and enlighten the women of Hell House that I will not be returning. All the best, ladies. All the best. Have fun with it.

Dolores came down to visit her mother and had her sign some checks for bill payments, around 11:30. She only spoke to me after I said, "Good morning," five minutes in. She had undertones of a "bad mood." Dolores tried calling one creditor to dispute a bill, but could not get through... She kept calling directory assistance and was told the number she called is the only one listed. After she left, I gently mentioned to Roxanne there was likely no answer because today is Sunday. She said, "No, this is Monday — Dolores said so."

I said (again, gently and carefully – almost whispering), "No, it's Sunday."

"OH," she mumbled, "That's why there was no answer."

Dolores moved some crap around near the wood-burning stove. I had a log sitting out to the side, which she positioned inside one container — which meant I could not remove the poker the next time I needed to add the log. I cannot tell whether that hogwash is on purpose or just because of her distractions. WHATever. I *do* know that I don't like her and I don't trust her — ever since she said to me, "Well, maybe you need to find something else." I'll never forget that. I'm holding that one in my back pocket. She knows how much I hate snow and cannot drive in it, so she mentions we're supposed to get another snowfall. But, this time, I don't take the bait — I say nothing in response. I just diverted my eyes as she glared at me and made myself look busy.

I see also that Dolores moved the location of Roxanne's unread books; for six weeks they sat on the dining room table, within her mother's reach. But now they are repositioned on the shelf beside Roxanne's wheelchair in the kitchen. Nice of her to let *me* know since I spend more time with her mother than she does. Again, I feel she is purposefully baiting me — pushing my buttons. But *why?* She knows that her mother cannot wheel her wheelchair around to access those books, and I cannot access them when Roxanne is in her wheelchair at the table without having her disengage the brakes on the chair and pulling her back while I retrieve whatever books she wants.

Also, whenever I try to make Roxanne smile — joke with her, or tease, Dolores clearly disapproves. I have tried to be the better person and interact more with Roxanne, but when Dolores is here, she seems to enjoy pushing me *and* her mother to negativity. She oddly resents effective communication or seeing her mother happy for a moment. Bizarre.

Matthew seems to think I should get out as soon as I am capable. I think I need to bank a little more money before running off to pay my own rent & groceries. I will chart that out later and determine whether I could function. I'm not afraid of tight finances, and I've got a longstanding history of being okay with sacrifice — especially where my son is concerned.

Roxanne has been tolerable & actually pleasant today; respectful, slightly sad, and her usual tired and cold self (currently, we are at 96 degrees Fahrenheit inside the house)... When I was putting her down for her nap, she made a comment about how she was a burden on Dolores... and said, "Sometimes it's easier to have strangers take care of you than your own family." I felt pity for her, but it would be short-lived.

I feel like a human roller coaster.

Dolores arrived to visit at 7:10. She had her classic impertinent undertone, as usual. She asked her mother if she had eaten all her dinner, and Roxanne whined (as though she was afraid), "Yes."

I added, in Roxanne's defense, "Yes! She ate everything. We had pork roast, potatoes, broccoli & noodles."

In a lovely patronizing response, she told me, "Hmmm... interesting"... not a compliment.

She also made a remark that Roxanne wanted cake and frosting. I said, "We have cake!"

"But do you have *frosting*?" Again, I recognize she is strategically and purposefully trying to make me feel everything I do is inadequate. SO SO SICK OF THIS SHIT. I politely offered her a piece of cake (with frosting) and she snarled, "No, I had cookies, but I didn't bring you any; you said you didn't want anything with sugar. Mom, at least she's still making dessert for you."

What a despicable troll. I have had absolutely enough of this trifling nonsense.

Also, she asked Roxanne, in her bullying tone, "Did you have your cranberry juice at dinner tonight?" Roxanne whined, "I don't know — I can't remember — ask *her* (pointing at me)." Dolores did *not* ask me; instead, she got up and poured a glass of cranberry juice and made her mother take it down. What a miserable, cruel, power-tripping, elder-abusive troll. Not my circus, not my monkeys, though — I need to let it go. After all, I am not the jackass whisperer.

Later, in the kitchen, Dolores repeated the cranberry narrative to me; I simply looked at her and then turned around. I had no intention of taking that bait, either. Roxanne *had* her cranberry juice, but it's my circus. I honestly no longer care.

I mention to Roxanne after Dolores left: "By the way, you *did you* have your cranberry juice tonight."

She replied, "I *told* her to ask you."

I merely said, softly, "Well, she didn't."

She added, "Well, I guess it won't hurt me."

She is emotionally abused, too. She told me how Lillian (her now deceased daughter) and Dolores did not get along. She has frequently spoken of how Lillian was a *piece of work* and that she is now dead. What a twisted, toxic family dynamic. They have no respect for life. This has been less than entertaining, but wildly educational.

I am also sick and tired of putting up with the dog's incessant whining and wanting to go out 11x today. Yes, I count — largely because I am daily accused of shirking duties, not doing enough... I document everything.

I don't see how I can continue in this position (or keep *assuming* the position) beyond March. I've had quite enough of this, and it is keeping me sad, irritated (I remember Mattie's assessment of "mad-sad disease" a while back when I was bullied in the Surrey law firm), and filled with anxiety on the best of days. Those "best of days" are merely the lesser of the evils projected. There *are* no good days here; case in point, today was one of the best in a long time. Things were tolerable, and as they should be — until Dolores set foot inside the house.

I am going to trust my intuition now; I keep internally questioning myself, doubting I see *what I truly feel I see* with Dolores — but it surfaces time and time again... And bottom line, Matthew despises her... My son feels that way about very FEW people. For his father, he feels that. He feels it for some of the particularly negligent caregiving experiences to which he was exposed — but really, no one else. He feels it for the woman who bullied me so relentlessly in the Surrey law firm, too — there he saw me stressed to the point of considering suicide.

I must be *very* careful because I also have observed that Dolores is vindictive. I must rent my apartment and put in an address change to Canada Post and Canada Revenue Agency right away, to stop any of my personal mail from coming here. There is zero possibility they would either forward or inform me anything had arrived. I trust Dave, but he has no key to the mailbox; Dolores keeps that under her control.

I will give no indicators that I am leaving... hopefully, I can manage an escape plan for Tuesday, February 28th (payday). Worst-case scenario, at the *very* latest, I want to be out of here by or before Friday, March 31st. In the grand scheme of things and how they turn on a dime here at Hell House, I don't even know if I can make it that far. But it's too cold to sleep in my car.

JANUARY 9, 2017

I awoke this morning, filled with anxiety — dreading any interaction with Dolores. My gut intuition *never* fails to me... *never* serves me incorrectly. I just tend to have no faith in my own abilities to understand, since it is so mind-boggling that circumstances are as they are in this household. Dolores is the reason I will need to leave, sooner than later. On arising, I could not distract myself from reliving her underhanded, button-pushing commentary last night.

Now at 6:38 AM, I need to go wash my face and begin the day... starting with snow removal and deicer application for the back wheelchair ramp entry. I want Dave to see I am on that, and save him the effort. Dolores will never give credit for anything.

Oh, and Dolores *never once* expressed gratitude for the clothing passed on from Matt's wardrobe. I sent a leather jacket down for Dave, and Dolores told her mother it was for *her*! Dolores is 4 feet 11 inches tall; that jacket came down to below her knees and the arms almost as far, too. She *did,* however, comment that the shirts that fit Matt would never fit her; well, she could barely pull that jacket shut. What an entitled, self-righteous troll — assuming a 270-pound man's clothing was ever intended for her?

I really need to get myself out of here. Each day I am organizing a few more of my items; each day, I remove one of my glass baking containers out of the kitchen and into my plastic storage bins.

After clearing snow and applying de-icer to the wheelchair ramp and the three-foot-wide walkway, I note (again) that it has been a full month since the light went out on the back porch. I refuse to do that — it's Dave's job to do that stuff, not the housekeeper-cook/poop&pee-flusher's job. Clearly, they do not care that this presents an *Occupier's Liability* problem for them... and having me stand on a ladder on a snow-covered wheelchair ramp — well, *Occupier's Liability* is pretty clear on a fall from that change in employment commandments. Thankfully, the snow won't last much more than another month, in all likelihood.

Now, I have about 30 minutes of freedom until Roxanne awakens (but her breakfast, coffee, pills & juices are ready and the fire is crackling). Time to take another look online for rentals — just in case my income tax return monies deposit tomorrow.

I dressed Roxanne in one of her pink fleece tops — it was the one with the malfunctioning zipper. Dolores had removed it from the sewing room where I put it last week (after Roxanne instructed me to place it there). I mentioned that, and Roxanne told me to use some soap on the zipper. Nope, I am not repairing clothing here either. They just keep adding little items, and I am no longer standing for it.

I changed the sheets on the bed this morning. Dolores told me last week she would change them, but the same sheets were on that bed, and not wanting to be accused of indiscretions in my duties, I removed the plaid sheets and added the flowered sheets.

OF COURSE, when Dolores arrived this morning, she said she had changed the sheets, starting with an accusation posed to her mother. "Did you wet your bed again?" Dolores *insisted* she changed the sheets.

I told her, "The same sheets were there *last week*, so I couldn't tell. Since we have a lack of communication in some areas, I'm just making sure my job is done." She, of course, did not disguise her annoyance with me, but I didn't care.

She brought in more wood from outside (I'd brought in and stacked two buckets yesterday); she slammed it around to make sure we all heard it. I did not say thank you. It's not really my job, anyway.

If there is no extra money on my payroll on the 15th (for consideration in doing her morning items for her on my day off, and adding wood to the fire while she is out for the afternoon leaving her mother alone), I will stop doing those. NOT my job; NOT getting paid; NOT getting a thank you for it. DONE.

I witness so many superfluous inconsistencies here from Dolores... "Don't ask Roxanne what she wants to eat," then she tells me later that she deserves to have a choice. WTF. "Keep the fire going," but then she tells me not to tend the fire every

20 minutes (if I do not, it will go out, then both of them will complain about the fire extinguishing)... "Don't clean every day," but then Dolores will remark about something not done (or relive a story about how another past caregiver did not attend to it). "Don't do my morning chores on your day off — it's your day off," but then she arrives late and infers it is *expected,* offering no gratitude for it having been done for her.

AND ANOTHER TWIT-RESPONSE. I keep endeavoring to be the better person and render a smile or a kind word or a joke with Dolores. She popped in again around 11:30 today. I glanced up when preparing Roxanne's lunch, and BAM — there the troll was. I said lightly, "You're quieter than a church mouse!"

I spoke with a smile, using my "sweet voice.

I got a retort, "WELL, I KNOCKED!"

SO, I tried again. "Well, I guess the rest of us here are just deaf!" That was spoken lightly and with a little chuckle.

But once again, I received the bitchy retort, "I *told* you, I KNOCKED TWICE." Hmmm, she never knocks. Why would she start now? Don't kid a kidder, lady. Waddle on back up the hill; we don't need you down here.

WHATever. I damn well give up on this nonsense. Just as with women in a law firm, the minute you try to be nice, offer a smile and a joke, they *castigate* you again with a fury like they're getting paid for it — assuming you are weak.

I have had enough. Mattie is right; I need to exit sooner rather than later. In one sense, it is a shame — cause another $800 makes a HUGE difference in my lifestyle going forward... I *hope* I can make it a choice, and not a desperate necessity to put up and shut up. I would take immense pleasure in calmly and kindly telling Dolores, *"We've both tried this, and we should just cut our losses. This is too emotional and inconsistent for me, and clearly, it's not good for you either. I will be leaving tomorrow."* Ahhh, in a perfect world...

I've been trying to glean some insight into this bizarre family scenario here... remembering when I first drove up to interview... and Dolores telling me her brother, Bob (who ran the advert I answered; despite the ad saying to call, I emailed) had said, "Here's another one who can't read." Why would she even share that?

It would appear conclusive that they're all from the same sanctimonious, selfish and cruel tree... Also in that interview, I have to remember Dolores saying, "OH — I forgot to mention there's a dog here; hope that's not a deal breaker"... That after speaking to me by telephone, reciting the job and duties descriptions, and having me drive four hours from the Lower Mainland to outer Kamloops — an isolated area near Kamloops Lake in the middle of nowhere. Sneaky right from the start... Of course, she knew not to mention it — since two caregivers hated the dog and ignored her... Ahhh, hidden truths surface in fairly short order.

Roxanne has been sweet and enjoyable again today... but I just had to get up and take my salad to my room to eat as she fed the dog at the dinner table again. That is a total taboo from Dolores' stern protocols of "no feeding the dog at the dinner table" and leaves more of a mess on the floor for *me* to clean. Plus, the dog is old and does not tolerate table scraps — she vomits and frequently has diarrhea — and of course, that falls within *my* purview to clean up. Even as she gives the dog a piece of pork roast, she says, "Now don't get sick." Egads, I had to walk away.

Mattie and Desi are right — I need to leave this zoo sooner rather than later.

Dolores visited her mother around 7:28 this evening; I heard her read out loud the numbers for Roxanne's blood work; everything else discussed was muffled and secretive. I did not venture out to the kitchen, as there was no purpose in that. I had no interest in "socializing" (has this household *ever* been sociable?) and I didn't need to be there while she visited with Roxanne.

Dolores came to my room, where I sat at the computer with my door open, around 7:45. She asked if I was okay putting Roxanne to bed, and I said, "Of course." Then she added, "To bed at 8, lights out at 9."

I felt it was condescending; after all, "lights out at 9" has been the protocol for three weeks now. I said, "Yes, just like every night." She asked if I was leaving tomorrow and I said yes. She asked what time, and I said I would leave at 10 when the bath girl arrived, and I'd be back before 2 PM. She said I could leave earlier, and I said, "Thank you, but business is business; I have a schedule and I'll leave at 10." She asked if we needed anything other than what I'd listed on the grocery list, and I said no.

I feel anxiety around her now, every time. I feel most of what she says is patronizing and strategized to bait me to response, anger, or frustration. I still cannot figure out *why*. Perhaps this is the first time any nominally paid caregiver has stood up to her oppression.

When I put Roxanne to bed, she asked what was wrong. I said I had anxiety. She asked why, and I told her I was not comfortable around Dolores for the past three days. She pressed for why and I told her. I said I felt I was talked to as though I was a kid, as though I was stupid, and with undertones at every turn. We had a LONG talk; unfortunately, she is going to broach this with Dolores — and I cannot see that going well. Apparently, BOTH of them are worrying I will leave, but I told Roxanne that "the tone" is pushing me right out the door. I live my life in peace and I simply will tolerate nothing that is encircled by confrontation and anxiety. She said, "Dolores has never had someone here with your nervous condition. You don't seem to like leaving doors unlocked here, even when you're told to do that."

"Don't blame this situation on my health. There are real issues here — BIG issues, and it is not new. You know that all too well, Roxanne."

There's my affirmation again; this is going nowhere — and fast. I need to vacate, sooner rather than later. I cannot relax with this, I cannot be healthy like this. My health is declining, I have gained weight (because I have no access to exercise and because I am stress-eating). There is *nothing* good about this for me. As nominal as the $800 per month is, it would make a significant difference in establishing a private apartment. However, the fact remains that if I am grossly unhappy, I will have great difficulty pulling myself together to go back to work.

I need to go — to move into private accommodation, with *my possessions*... get back to the gym... relax, and get my head on straight to write — and ultimately, to return to work in law for mid-summer.

JANUARY 10, 2017

Cheryl was the bath attendant today; awesome gal. I gave her the red Columbia Ski Jacket, and she was thrilled. It fit her perfectly.

I left at 10 and returned at 1:50. Today, I picked up Mattie, and we had lunch with Angela and Wilhelm. Awesome time spent — and they both agreed I need to get out of this situation.

I spoke with the on-site manager of an apartment building on the North Shore and made an appointment to see it on Thursday at 10. He warned me first-come/first-serve — anyone comes with a deposit, it'll be gone. I reconsidered, double-checked with Dolores by phone, and opted to take Wednesday and Thursday as my days off. After picking up Mattie at 8:30, I will pay a deposit on the place if it is remotely acceptable. I suspect it will be fine — especially considering what I live with right now.

Came back feeling refreshed & great... Got Roxanne up at 5, gave her dinner, and both of us enjoyed a good mood until Dolores arrived with groceries. I tried the good-mood response, but once she was inside the house, she was barking orders again.

"You can give Gramma rice pudding and some ice cream." She stood there *waiting* for me to perform (I was putting away groceries). It pissed me off, and I asked if I could do this on my own time — adding I would get the snack in one minute. What I *wanted to say*, but kept inside my head, would have been to do it herself, if it was so critically urgent.

She gave a sour face and shrugged, and I could tell she was walking on eggshells. Then, she came back (after I provided the snack) and asked me to put the teapot in the microwave for one minute. I finished putting what I had in my hand away first and then put the fucking teapot in the microwave. OH WOW — invariably, when I think I can make this work, she gets under my skin all over again.

THEN, "What time are you leaving in the morning? 8 o'clock?" I said, "No, I'm exiting around 7:30 in the morning."

The troll replied, "Well, that's alright you don't have to wait until I get here." YA THINK? WTF. So I said, gently but matter-of-factly, "It's my day off, I can leave any time I need to." I decided at that moment, but kept the decision to myself, that when the time came that I *was* vacating Hell House, I would not stay through the night; I would put Roxanne to bed, ensure she was asleep — and exit thereafter. The protocol has always been that Roxanne could telephone Dolores in an emergency; actually, before I agreed to accept this position (hmmm, more like *assume the position*), that was how they managed for months.

She replied with a tone, "Yeah, that's right."

Darn skippy, it's right.

In my personal business again, she queries if I am bringing Mattie back tomorrow. We go through this every miserable week. I replied, "Yes, Matt will be with me on *every* day off, as we discussed, and as you approved."

"Well, that's alright." I thought (but also kept this one inside my head) — wow, do I really need to thank your fat ass every time? NOT going to do it. And I didn't.

Since it is one of my itemized duties to keep Dolores informed about grocery needs, I mentioned to her that we need more eggs and she retorted, "I brought down a dozen earlier." For eight consecutive miserable weeks, we have kept eggs on the 2nd left shelf; she began that protocol and I followed suit. *Now*, she puts the eggs on the top shelf of an over-stuffed fridge? ABSOLUTELY ON PURPOSE, but *why?* Is Dolores the one suffering from early-onset Alzheimer's?

MAKING A LIST & CHECKING IT TWICE

M y financial quandary continues as the plot thickens. Do I stick it out through February for another $800? That will make a significant difference in my budget, but if it is going to rob me of sanity, balance, and quality of life, I'm not sure if it is worth $800. Things are getting *that bad* for me now. If Dolores would just stay away, or keep her trap shut and leave the baiting in the fish pond where it belongs, I might be able to manage Roxanne. Can she not see she is pushing me *right out the door?* She will have this load on her back again shortly. For an educated, retired registered nurse, I query how she survived that profession — as I don't see a litany of intelligence portrayed here.

I find myself dismayed by this low level of income and my resulting desperation because of it. Heck, I earned more than this when I accepted my first job at 16.

Since tomorrow is my day off, I started doing the prep work for the next morning; I put out the morning & noon meds, and pulled out the glasses for juices & the coffee cup for Roxanne, and then STOPPED MYSELF. What is wrong with me?

I put the glasses and coffee cup back. I am doing *nothing* tomorrow morning... no juices out; no pre-made porridge... no ashes removed from the wood stove and no fire started. Here's the start of Dolores learning a lesson about how she cannot expect me to remain a belittled and abused servant. Niceties extended are taken for granted and are now expected, and I am DONE. I am no longer trapped; I have a plan — although I am going to let her continue to think I am stuck.

JANUARY 11, 2017

Realized as I was quietly getting ready how stressed I am on awakening here... sneaking around so as not to wake up the dog and starting that demanding w hine-fest... making sure I leave none of my notes for her to ramble through and nose around (I can tell when my things have been moved, and they are disturbed frequently: my storage crates, my trunk, which she damaged and for which no apology was forthcoming). It has been a continuing and infuriating invasion of privacy. It's left me feeling like a criminal sneaking out of the house quietly, avoiding the areas on the floor that creak.

Just another chapter of Wednesday Weirdness!

I am off to get gas, pick up two extra-large Timmy's dark roasts, and Matt — and will leave at the crack of dawn. I did *nothing* for the wenches of Hell House. Dolores can perform her own morning protocols. It's her job, so she can get used to it again.

I am confident she will leave a mess for me to clean up, but WHATever. There's not much more of this left to endure, thankfully. I truly need 30-60 days to deprogram from all this... get back to the gym and back to eating *my* way. And just like that, Frank Sinatra's son is stuck in my head!

When I tried to pull out of the driveway, the snow/ice had not been cleared for some time, so it took me 20 minutes of rocking my car backward and forward for 20 minutes to exit the heavily snowed driveway. I was told repeatedly that they would clear the driveway for ease of exit on my days off. I am confident this was purposeful as well. Certainly, no one from the health authority would attempt to scale that incline with about 19 inches of fresh snow on the ground. This will be another reason to exit.

JANUARY 12, 2017: Second Day Off

When I returned with Mattie yesterday, they had cleared the driveway of snow and de-iced.

This morning, Mattie and I were out at the crack of dawn to deliver another carload to the apartment. I left a note for Dolores saying we'd be back a couple of times to take more loads to storage at my friends' garage.

When we returned for the next load, Dolores greeted me in the mudroom, gave me my wages early, and said it was ridiculous I was moving my things out of the room. She was furious. I simply said, "Let's not be negative." She continued, saying she was *shocked*... I repeated, "No negativity." I continued on my way, demonstrating that her words meant nothing to me now, and she turned around and stormed out of the mudroom. I was enraged, but I did not show it.

In any event, she did not bother me for the next three trips... On trip #5 (around 2:15 PM) she was leaving to return to her place, and surprisingly, she was sweet as day-old excrement. Matt was there and was stunned. Could this be a good sign? If she returns to her usual demeanor, I will leave without notice, at the end of this month. One day at a time. We'll see. I am not "holding my breath."

I suspect she reconsidered, knowing *not* I had no heavy ties to the place or to enduring abuse and disrespect. If I have friends who will give me a key to their garage and let me store my belongings, I have friends that might put me up (in her mind). And my background will provide me with a job in law, in short order.

As the bottom line, there is no reason for her to continue bullying me, and if she does, I will leave her high and dry. She *says* she does not want to provide full-time care for her mother; *says* it is too much for her; *says* Dave wants me to stay; *says* Roxanne wants me to stay. I know I have done *nothing* wrong. I have an excellent work ethic and I am dependable. I know I am a good cook; I keep a very clean home... Now, at least, they know I will accept no further nonsense. Perhaps, therefore, her attitude has improved.

I see Dolores has noted extras to the grocery list, and at the *end* of the list, she has added "water plants; mop floors." Does that mean she is changing the Wednesday watering schedule that I have done for eight consecutive weeks and annotated on my reporting list to her (posted to the kitchen cabinet) or that she did this on one of my days off? And is she commanding me to mop floors, or communicating that she did this?

I will have to speak with her personally to clarify this; we have very poor communications ongoing. I would rather not speak, and just try to figure it out on my own. Guaranteed, there will be conflict — as that is what she does best and enjoys most, now.

> Making my own list and checking it twice,
> 'Cause at Hell House, all are naughty — not nice!

DANCING A SIDE STEP

W ell, my first train of thought was that we have trouble in paradise again... but the group home has not been paradise since late November 2016. Things continue to be "in transition" at the home, and Matthew's distractions and behaviors continue to alter in his time there. I am deeply concerned, particularly as my own situation is so dire and inflexible at present.

Today, I received a request by email from the new manager of the facility.

> We are hoping to have a meeting with yourself in the next 2 weeks and then a care conference with yourself and Matt. I will contact our case manager for her availability. We have not met as a group in person And it would be great do so. Thank you.

JANUARY 13, 2017

Mattie has asked me to take him to see "Moonlight" next! His gift certificate and his Access 2 Entertainment card will be very well used! When the movie was released, however, Matthew did not want to see it. He often refused to see success stories achieved by others; he usually took a stance of finding fault — jealousy, undoubtedly, that always fed his insecurities and diminished his opportunity to be the center of attention.

There's been more communication with the group home's new management, after being told by them that the meeting requested might not be attended by the case manager from the health authority. Not a chance of that. That would be like speaking to a Defense counsel as a Plaintiff with no lawyer. I asked that a date be accommodated when both the group home management could attend *with* Matthew's case manager from the health authority.

My email to the group home manager, copied to the health authority, included a commentary as follows.

> Again, I feel it is appropriate for all meetings to occur with our case manager present; it has been this way for two and one-half years and there should be no reason to change that. Thank you for understanding.

> I will pick up Matt on Tuesday at our usual 11 AM, returning him around 1:15. I will pick up Matt on Thursday around 8:30 AM, as usual, and return him before dinner on Friday. In a couple of weeks, I will begin taking Matt to the gym for exercise — as he has not received exercise since Angela was director of the home, despite that having been addressed in the last teleconference. For now, I have time in my schedule to get him to the gym for exercise twice a week. He will also eat clean while with me, as his weight has been slowly rising again.

> Could you also provide an update on whether his BC ID will be replaced? I have received no response to my prior inquiries. If you need a copy of those emails again, please let me know — and I will resend them. I confirm the health authority was copied with that. One of your staff advised, by email, two weeks ago that she was to take him to get a replacement card.

> Thank you.

THEN, my next communication – email to the health authority case manager, *not copied* to the group home management.

PRIVATE & CONFIDENTIAL

Regarding the email from the manager of Matthew's group home residence below, please note that my only available time for an in-person meeting would be on a Wednesday, Thursday, or Friday — and I need to arrange that one week in advance.

Another telephone conference would work just as well, in my unsolicited opinion. I have found new management to be confrontational and difficult in communications, and the tone of voice used by the new manager, in our last teleconference, concerned me as well. I recorded that conversation, as you know.

I suffer from C-PTSD, and it is easily triggered by confrontation. I want to ensure there will be no conflict in a face-to-face meeting, and I am unclear why that is necessary.

My days for attendance will be limited to a Wednesday, Thursday, or Friday if we *must* attend face-to-face, and I need to arrange that one week in advance. I cannot easily reschedule on short notice, either.

Because this is *Matthew's life*, I ask that he be made a party to the meeting as well — whether in-person or by teleconference.

I thank you in advance for your anticipated understanding.

NEXT DANCE STEP, another email to group home management.

I need to insist that the health authority case manager be present at any meetings with the group home. I also believe Matthew should be present. If there is some item you wish to broach in his absence, we could cover that in the initial portion of the meeting, and permit him entry thereafter. I prefer to *not* have two separate meetings/on separate dates.

I agree another teleconference is in order, but am unsure why a face-to-face meeting is "necessary." If I must attend in person, my only available dates/times would be a morning on Wednesday, Thursday, or Friday — and I will need one week in advance to schedule that. Once scheduled, I cannot re–book on short notice.

If there are other issues to which I need to be privy, I ask that you email me in advance so that I am prepared — and not *broadsided* — at an important meeting. Efficiency needs to be paramount for all of us.

Thanks in advance,

Sarah Martin

Hi Sarah,
I will speak with the case manager regarding a timeline for the upcoming meetings, as it is important for us to meet as a team for the care of Matthew. I would expect both meetings to happen on the same day. **We all have very busy lives**.

But wait, there *IS* more. Still another email (glad I asked for that — since these things cannot be left to simmer and stew) from the group home manager, telling me there had been an incident in the group home where Matthew was bullying another resident.

Yikes. He can't take any more where he is, and I cannot endure more where I am. I am so grateful he only saw one indiscretion at Hell House, and everything else has been camouflaged from him. I have protected him from that. He has enough going on in trying to deal with the painful transitions in the best group home he has ever known — until late November last year, anyway.

SO, still more communications. I wonder what any of us did before emails and the internet. Sure, I'm old enough to remember — but I cannot imagine living effectively without modern technology.

This time, a phone call was in order. I telephoned to speak with my son. Knowing his anxiety levels were off the charts right now, I was gentle but communicated succinctly.

He apologized, said he understood — said things were terrible at his home, and he would just try to keep to his room, stay away from people that made him want to act out. He continued,

> "I understand, Mom. I really get it. I am truly sorry. I will be better. But I hate it here so much. It is so not the same as it was when Angela was here."

We ended the conversation with an "I love you." He asked if he could still call me tonight, and I told him, "Absolutely, Buddy — I look forward to it!"

Whew, then still another email to group home management.

> As promised, I had a word with Matt about ten minutes ago.

> I referenced the bullying over the TV remote that he did with Paul, and he admitted to it. He said he had apologized to Paul, and I reminded him (firmly but gently) that apologies don't erase the infraction or the memory of it. I reminded him of the analogy of crumpling a paper — we can straighten it out, but it is forever changed.

> I reminded him to be more respectful with staff, no matter WHAT stress or attitude he perceives from anyone. I reminded him that the job is not a cakewalk for any staff on the best of days and that he should have a goal of being the best resident there, respect staff, and set an example for other residents that might be less high-functioning or more problematic with him. He told me he understood.

I try, now, to appeal to his "adult" sense of setting examples, rather than his brat-teenager side that surfaces. It takes time to know what works with Matt, and it's always subject to change without notice, but I keep trying this angle...

I also mentioned the money with which he was found. I told him I did not want to hear any excuses — he was *never* to have money on his person. He is *never* to enter my car with money wanting to treat me to coffee (this has happened, and he's told me he got money from his fund/from staff). I told him this is not allowed.

He tried to object, and I told him he needed to keep an excess few dollars in his fund in case of a dental emergency — and I reminded him if this happens, I can no longer fund dental care as I did in the past. He said he forgot about that, of course, and I reminded him why he would always need supervision in his life.

He told me he had sold a couple of cigarettes to residents, and I told him I did not believe him. I told him this was forbidden, and he knew better; if he DID this, he would run short of smokes, and would then ask for more from staff — and this was a negative, vicious circle that did NOTHING good for anyone. He again expressed understanding. I reinforced this firmly, telling him I would tolerate no bullshit (sorry, my exact words — sometimes I have to be more descriptive with Matt when he really needs to remember something). I told him if he EVER entered my car/had a visit with me with cash, he would be returned to the group home and the visit would end. NO excuses, no exceptions, and I asked if he understood. He said he did.

He told me he was going to apologize to you.

I also told him he must come to me better groomed (e.g., to trim that goatee and to take responsibility for his appearance; he has a beard trimmer, and to use it; I told him I was embarrassed by his lack of grooming; he concurred he had been lazy).

He also came out without gloves and a toque. He was told to come out prepared next time. It was part of adult responsibility to be more prepared than a child would be. I gave him my toque to wear, and he needs to return that to me, as it is my only headgear right now for the winter cold. I also bought him another cheap pair of gloves.

We discussed, again, that in two more weeks, he would go to the YMCA with me and he would weight train again. He said he would, and I said the hot tub would be his reward, but I expected a minimum of 20 minutes on the gym floor with me!

Whew, I think that's about it. Just wanted to bring you up-to-date on what I've said to him!

Thanks again.

And to conclude with the return email from group home management: "Thank you for the update. Matt apologized to myself and the other client."

Another crisis diverted for now. The side-step dance can continue another day, but for now, we are back in rhythm.

MOVIN' ON UP (OR AT LEAST OUT)

Now January 14, 2017 — and I have set some very strong boundaries of late, and moved all my personal effects out, under the guise of placing them into storage, but in reality, I have now secretly rented an inexpensive apartment of my own in the city. On my two days away from the client, I will stay in my own space overnight — and have Mattie there with me.

We will begin cleaning and unpacking next week, and get all set up; grateful I suffered through bringing my personal effects up here with me, to start over from nothing, still again, would have been impossible.

So now, I have a "10-strikes you're out" list. Every time I am confronted or bullied or slave-handled with more duties (which I refuse now), I put it on my list. The list began January 12 (the date I got the keys to my apartment) and already there are 3 strikes... but I can say affirmatively, that is a *significant* improvement. They've both smartened up and are walking on eggshells with me since I moved my belongings out (the daughter confronted me very strongly in front of my son — raised her voice... and my only response (twice) was "Hey, no negativity, right?") She ultimately walked away, but not before putting Matt into tears over the confrontation with me for no reason. Glad he is saddened these days rather than angered. None of us need to see anger and aggression from a 270 lb, 6'3" 38-year-old young man with a history of martial arts, boxing, and sports. Thank goodness, my young man has adopted the lessons of tolerance and gentility put his way since the traumatic brain injury, with remarkable success through six of those 15 years... and no, it has not always been a "cakewalk."

He told me how surprised he was that I kept my cool and rose above. "Mom, you were the better person. She was baiting you — and YOU KNOW I recognize that, because I am so good at it, or at least I used to be. I sure hope I am not that person anymore, but I know the old Matt is just under the surface. I don't wanna bug him. I am really and truly in *awe* of you — how much you put up with and still keep your composure — is that the right word? It sounds good, but I'm not sure. I like that word, 'composure.'"

And I took the learning opportunity to teach him a new phrase, "composure in the face of adversity.'

"THAT's EXACTLY what you had, Mom! Composure in the diversity — right?"

"Composure in the face of adversity, buddy."

He repeated and got it right this time, and I wondered if he would commit it to memory. "Composure in the face of adversity."

So, there's a light at the end of the tunnel, and I'm hoping there's no train. I'm keeping my cool, proceeding with professional resolve and I will return to the gym in two weeks, hopeful to return to genuine work in eight weeks, but need my head on straight first with some downtime. That is also all strategized on paper, with three different alternative solutions.

Use EVERYTHING as an opportunity to understand, grow and expand, while you've still got your head screwed on reasonably straight.

JANUARY 14, 2017

Tonight's dinner: roasted beets with caramelized onions, feta & pecans; beet greens cooked in chicken broth with garlic; baked salmon. Thought I'd provide the recipe. After all, I talk too much about the meals I've been preparing and maybe anyone reading thinks I'm just writing tales!

ROASTED BEETS WITH CARMELIZED ONIONS, FETA & PECANS
- 2 tbsp organic apple cider vinegar
- 2 tsp coarse Dijon mustard
- 1 tsp sea salt
- 1 tsp garlic-sesame spice
- Black pepper
- 3 tbsp coconut oil or avocado oil
- 1lb sweet yellow onion (chopped)
- ½ tsp dark brown sugar
- 15 whole fresh small beets peeled & roasted
- 4 oz crumbled feta cheese (or to taste)
- Toasted pecans (or walnuts)

Directions
Quarter the beets if they are large, if they are small, then just cut them in half.

In a large bowl, whisk together cider vinegar, Dijon mustard, black pepper, and salt.

In a slow steady stream, whisk in 3 tablespoons olive oil whisking continuously until well combined.

In a large fry pan, cook the sweet onions in about 3-4 tablespoons of coconut (or avocado) oil with ½ tsp brown sugar until golden brown (about 15-18 minutes, until caramelized); season with salt and pepper to taste.

Add the cooked beets, caramelized onions, and feta cheese to the bowl; stir gently to combine.

Sprinkle with toasted pecans (or walnuts, or sliced almonds)

Roxanne has been in a good mood this morning; good communications.

Dolores rolled in unannounced around 10:45 AM, no good mornings, no hello.

For a fleeting moment, my crazed brain considers whether she has audio-video at her place, watching and listening to everything we do down here. Like clockwork, on those rare occasions when Roxanne has been pleasant, cordial, and wanting to communicate — *invariably,* Dolores trudges in and sucks the life out of the room.

"Have you been to the bathroom?" The tone left me feeling (or worrying) I had done something wrong, but I was merely washing dishes after giving Roxanne her mid-morning snack. Besides, I don't make extra work or invite ill-treatment for myself by taking her to the washroom if she doesn't ask for it.

So, Dolores rolls her around to the bathroom and again asks, but more emphatically and dramatically, "Did you take a dump yesterday?" Roxanne meekly says yes.

Dolores turns to me, with a demandingly inquiring facial expression, and I mouth silently, "No."

She shames her mother, "You took a shit the day before yesterday, not yesterday — and *not* today."

How crass, how inappropriate, how unsympathetic. How disrespectful. It's not physical, but it certainly *is* elder abuse.

She returns Roxanne to the kitchen, adding "You can dump that commode now", as I am tending the fire, and she slinks into the kitchen to the sink. I *know* there are no dishes, but when I walk around the corner to prepare Roxanne's lunch, she says, "OH! YOU CAUGHT ME WASHING DISHES."

I merely said, "Well, I know I didn't leave any."

She sheepishly said, "No, you didn't — I'm just washing Gramma's little bowl from her morning snack." WHATEVER. I had put some three-inch bandages on the shopping list and Dolores curtly went to the cabinet (which I've never opened, as it is not my place to snoop and if I *did*, I would never hear the end of it) and she tells enlightens me. "We have plenty." Then she promptly closes the cabinet.

"Well, we don't have any inside Roxanne's nightstand." So I opened the cabinet again and took half of them, saying, "I'll transfer those to the bedroom so I didn't forget." She thoroughly enjoys being sneaky. She *loves* to miscommunicate and then *loves* to trip me up. It is undeniable.

After that, she waddles over to the wood-burning stove, opens the door, and pokes at it. It's just fine, and there's no room for another log. She is just pushing buttons. I won't include this petty nonsense on my list of "strikes out", but it is annoying. I despise this woman. She is assuredly walking on eggshells with me, as my replies are professional but matter-of-fact and even cold. I am not her friend, nor is she mine. *The minute* I let my guard down, she attacks. I'm not leaving myself exposed to that anymore. Business — straight business.

Be unprofessional and abusive with me, and I'm done and gone on a payday, with no notice, no warning — but definitely with a toothy SMILE!

After Dolores left, Roxanne asked me, "What did Dolores do with that patch she took over to that table?" She pointed toward the living room.

I told her, "I have no idea — she doesn't communicate much with me, and I ask nothing because I want to avoid confrontation at all costs; I've had enough, Roxanne."

Roxanne *wanted* to say something, but she stopped herself. She looked sad, however, which tells me (1) she understands and knows FULL WELL what is going on, and (2) she does not want to jeopardize pissing me off.

Then, at 12:20, after I brought in two more buckets of wood, Roxanne says, "You'll wanna close the damper or you'll burn up more wood." WHATEVER. I reduced the damper again, but not completely because I don't want to deal with a fire fully expiring and have to contend with the bitchery guaranteed to follow, judging how I let a fire go out. Then, she adds, with a bit of a whine, "I know I'm being bossy." I said nothing and made no eye contact. My way of acknowledging that she knows precisely what she is doing. Had I offered a comment or kindness, I would be raked over the coals with her next lineup of oddities and curiosities.

Whew. This place is exhausting.

5:15 PM

Dinner is served. I sat the dinner down and she looked annoyed as she picked at the beets and said, "Is this bacon?"

"BEETS — remember, I told you earlier I was baking fresh beets with greens and baking salmon. You told me you love beets." She picked at it with her fork some more, picked at the salmon, and I took a knife and easily broke it up for her, in case she was struggling with that. Then, when she tossed a chunk of salmon down on the floor (in response to the dog begging at the dinner table, I was sufficiently annoyed to take my plate to my room, where I had dinner alone.

I wanted to share a beautiful note from a dear friend and her husband. I share this with her permission and at her suggestion, along with another photo of my beloved Mattie...

YES, the connection between a mother and son is assuredly a *different kind of relationship*, but the whys, wherefores, and realities are absolutely the same. The photo of Mattie is during one of his visits home. This was one of our most difficult survival times; the horrors of traumatic brain injury and wrongful medication rendered him institutionalized for an 18-month term at that time. It took a toll on both of us but we worked through it, with no regrets.

Lifelong commitment is not what everyone thinks it is. It's not waking up early every morning to make breakfast and eat together. It's not cuddling in bed together until both of you peacefully fall asleep. It's not a clean home and a homemade meal every day. It's someone who steals all the covers. It's sometimes slammed doors, a few harsh words, disagreeing, and the silent treatment until your hearts heal. Then... forgiveness! It's coming home to the same person every day that you know loves and cares about you, in spite of (and because of) who you are. It's laughing about the times you accidentally did something stupid. It's about dirty laundry and unmade beds without finger-pointing. It's about helping each other with the hard work of life! It's about swallowing the nagging words instead of saying them out loud. It's about the cheapest and easiest meal you can make and sitting down together at 10 PM to eat because you both had a crazy day. It's when you have an emotional breakdown, and your love lays with you and holds you and tells you everything is going to be okay, and you believe them. It's when "Netflix and chill" literally means you watch Netflix and hang out. It's about still loving someone even though sometimes they make you absolutely insane. Living with the person you love is not perfect, and sometimes it's hard, but it's amazing and comforting and one of the best things you'll ever experience.

PONDERING **PTSD**

I have a lot of folks who look confused when they hear me mention my C-PTSD diagnosis. I recently realized a very large majority have NO IDEA what PTSD is. It certainly affects its victims in many similar ways, as does a stroke or a brain injury, but with various and assorted diverse and unpredictable mechanisms. C (complex) PTSD is the PTSD condition amalgamating over years of multiple and serious traumas, with even small stressors contributing after a point. And I can tell you, after voluminous research, there are few psychiatrists and psychologists truly qualified to treat the malady. I have it on good authority there is only one psychiatrist in Kamloops that is "worth their salt" for this *niche-market* diagnosis and treatment. Like all other physicians here, no one is even accepting names for a waitlist, and no one is open to a referral.

Matthew also suffers from C-PTSD. Sadly, his discussions with his psychiatrist are nominal — given his inability to remember or communicate effectively. I believe the PTSD conditions and realities are overlooked in the course of Matthew's TBI transitions.

Complex PTSD is trauma layered on trauma, layered on trauma. It often will start with childhood sexual, emotional, or physical abuse, move into personal violations experienced as teens, and continue into adulthood traumas. Having the response to trauma that is typical of PTSD makes a person more likely to have a PTSD response again. PTSD alters our brain – and alters it over and over again.

What *is* a PTSD response to trauma? It is when the amygdala (our emotional processing center in our brains, sometimes called our "fight or flight control center") reacts to what would be normal 'trauma' by responding as if this is THE BIG ONE. When that happens, it shoots out massive amounts of cortisol, which expedites delivery next door to the hippocampus and covers it (like swiss cheese —

with 'holes' in the covering). The hippocampus is where we store our memories... and the cortisol 'protects' our memories from overwhelming events by creating this 'blanketed' covering. *Some* memories get into the hippocampus, many do not. But the fact remains: they are there!

The 'other' memories deposit inside our cells; it's an apt storage facility, another reminder of the remarkable creation we take for granted with our human body... We often hear that called 'cellular' memory. That cellular memory shows up when something happens that reminds our 'body' of the past (singular or plural) BIG ONE(s). We respond as if the trauma is happening right here, right now... and it can be so convincingly insistent that we feel there is nothing we can do about it [often we feel death is our only solace; death can be our only peaceful freedom]. We find ourselves on the side of the road in our cars — belly crying — and unable to stop. We often respond to otherwise trivial life occurrences in the most intense of ways.

For example, In my case, a knock on the door can become an intense trigger. I have learned that a knock on the door is not good news. My memories recall violence from my husband that began with him pounding on my door when impaired by alcohol or drugs. My memories include hiding from him behind a locked door, and him taking that door off its hinges to come after me. Trips to the hospital frequently ensued, and the 9-1-1 dispatch grew to recognize my voice on incoming calls in the early years in Ontario.

All this, collectively, is why the condition is permanent — and very difficult to treat. Often, those that are too "worn down" or lesser capable of researching and intellectually understanding what is going on in their bodies fall prey to debilitation. Many commit suicide, simply being horrified and tired of being incapable of socializing, and interacting well in the community, and in the workplace — particularly during situations of political rhetoric involving insecure individuals (those with PTSD often develop a "Type A" personality, as their work ethic is often the only phenomenon that provides them with any esteem or self-worth/value. As a consequence, it becomes a permanent vicious circle that can only be navigated carefully, with great attentive focus, and repeatedly (countless times each day)).

Many of us (myself included) develop a "perfectionist" approach to everything we do... for the self-worth/value aspect of our limited lifestyles *and* to create a presentation that is less likely to elicit criticism or judgment from others. It is still another effort toward avoiding confrontation. We over-perform, we over-perform, we over-create, we over-compensate — all because we need the reinforcement from others that we are enough, that we exhibit quality work ethic and are dependable and committed to excellence... and when the recognition cannot come to pass, we lose *still more* from our supplies of self-worth and value. Our purpose becomes clouded and doubt prevents us from finding better ways forward.

And on top of all that, try being underpaid for your level of expertise and being bullied in the workplace? We invariably end up feeling that if we can do *everything* perfectly, then no one should critique or judge us... but alas, sometimes *that*, in and of itself, invites criticism from those who need to make themselves elevated by judging others, and the power-tripper thrives on the discomfort of others and their power over them.

AND SOMETIMES, it all gets to be just too much... the perpetuation of the abuse, the PTSD response to it, and not being able to visualize any end or resolution to the horrors... That's when PTSD drives depression and suicide becomes a logical response.

PTSD is not depression, but depression comprises one multitude of symptoms of PTSD. It is anxiety x100, it is paranoia personified, it is the belly of overthinking and over-analysis — as a protective mechanism, a survival mechanism, and to avoid confrontation and the "fight or flight" that invariably thrives repeatedly in this medium.

Post-Traumatic Stress Disorder entangles with a family of multiple other disorders, such as the dissociation that Matthew has exhibited, and such as the depression that has plagued me since my early teen years. I diligently watch for the signs of triggering with my son and try to recognize the warning signs in myself. Some indicators for which I remain apprehensive (for myself and for my son) include:

- Internalized reminders of a traumatic event, typically presenting as nightmares or flashbacks.
- Avoidance of external reminders, in Matthew's case — a complete inability to enter the city limits of Vancouver, traveling in the car with his eyes closed if our route takes us past Colony Farms or any prison facility, and more.
- We must recognize altered anxiety states; such changes can reflect an impending decompensation.
- Changes in mood or thinking are precursors to changes in behavior. Case in point, Matthew has been happy as a lark, thriving and improving, until new management changed structure and more in the group home. Changes in mood or train of thought are key to identifying and creating strategies to redirect disaster.

Post-Traumatic Stress Disorder (PTSD) is a psychiatric disorder that can occur in individuals who have experienced or witnessed a traumatic event — such as a natural disaster, a life-threatening event (or even the *perception* of a life-threatening event), a serious accident, a terrorist act, war and combat, rape, or who have had an "on the brink" experience with death, sexual violence, or serious injury. While it is potentially treatable, the treatment often involves more experimentation with medications (which can take on a life of itself, with complex interactions with other medications prescribed), an intense learning curve for the PTSD afflicted person, and with TBI — the strategies developed through cognitive-behavioral therapy, are more complicated because of altered brain activity.

Then, we could write books (a litany of others have) on how PTSD alters the brain. Throw in a dose of traumatic brain injury to the mix — and voila: recipe for disaster.

THE FORESHADOWING OF ABUSE

H alfway through January at Hell House now. January 15th.
       Roxanne has been in a good mood this morning; good conversation...
It makes me wonder whether Dolores will time her entry here, blazing in glory
for more sedition. Certainly the more she does that, the more my plan becomes
cemented.

Roxanne asked me over breakfast if I was bringing Matt out again next week and
I told her no. I would not be bringing him out again.

She snapped, "Why *NOT?*"

I reminded her how Dolores had wrongfully confronted me and disrespected
me in front of Matthew when I was moving my things out to storage. Roxanne
told me this was *her* fault because she assumed Dolores had told me to move my
things out.

I clarified that it was not remotely her fault, and EVEN IF (which I don't
believe for a minute) Dolores was of that opinion, she had no right to be so
confrontational and rude to me – especially in the presence of my son. "She
overstepped professional boundaries by a LONG shot; I will neither forget it nor
forgive it. I would *never* subject my sensitive, brain-injured son to that risk of
behavioral nonsense ever again."

"Well, you're cheating him out of a chance to come out here."

"Nice try, Roxanne. You're violating boundaries now. I cheat my son of nothing,
Roxanne — other than the risk of being triggered, explaining AGAIN that he was
shaking and crying after witnessing the shock of Dolores' tone and behavior that
day. "I protect my son and keep him from unnecessary drama, confrontation, and
triggers. I also will take *no risk* that he will be here to listen to one of Dolores'
stories about how she so callously let her brother die down here. I also would not want

him to see a calendar on the wall from a *funeral home*. He will not be returning here again. That is my decision, and it is not up for conjecture or negotiation, and discussions about my son will now cease."

She let it go and said nothing.

About an hour later, I mentioned I would make more rice pudding for her later today after Dolores brought more eggs. She told me to call her and let her know we were out of eggs.

Not wanting to make the call and enable another attack, I did not engage further on the subject with Roxanne. I've been educated to predict where *that* goes. I let ten minutes pass, however, and phoned Dolores — to remind her to call Eileen to wish her a happy birthday (as Roxanne had requested) and to mention in passing that we were out of eggs and I was going to make more rice pudding (as Roxanne had requested). From the time she answered the phone, it was apparent she was in another one of her typical crass and nasty moods.

I was reprimanded for mentioning Eileen's birthday. "As if it's any of your business. I called her yesterday." I could tell she did not welcome the call from me for the eggs. Education accepted, again: there will never be another call from me for any purpose other than a valid emergency, henceforth.

Clearly, Dolores would rather miscommunicate or relay messages to me via her forgetful, almost deaf mother — still another example of how she relishes and furthers confrontation, bossiness, bullying, and negativity. This one counts as another strike on the lack of communication front — as communications are entirely necessary and appropriate in a caregiving relationship.

11:15 AM

Darleen arrives with her traditional dark disposition and puts eggs on the counter. No hello, no courtesy, no smile. Nothing but her inimitable, brooding disparity.

She then wheels Roxanne down to the commode, which seems poised to make me feel I have done something wrong. Certainly, there's no denying that emotional abuse breeds insecurity in a victim. She does eventually ask me how things have been going (cold and perfunctory), and I reply in a monotone, "Things are great." A moment later, after giving me instructions to stop the Betadine applications to Roxanne's "sore crack" (of course, this is technical phrasing from a registered nurse — nice) and only to apply more zinc oxide before bed tonite, she hands Roxanne the lunch I pre-made earlier and then leaves, saying "Later" to her mother and nothing to me.

Darleen arrived around 7:35 PM. I had completed Roxanne's bloodwork and served her a snack at 7:10 PM. Roxanne had not touched her dessert, oddly — since she fights at every turn to have that as an appetizer.

"Eat your snack," Dolores commanded — not asking politely if her mother was feeling okay, or whether she preferred another snack.

These two women of Hell House! 'Ya can't make this stuff up! Roxanne interjects, pointing at me with a frail and crooked finger, "She just *brought* it."

Well, maybe Roxanne has no ability to discern the passing of time — 25 minutes in this case. Or more likely, perhaps I am the scapegoat because she fears her daughter's reprisal.

Dolores asked me how Roxanne's day had been, and I replied, "Fine." I can't help but consider that one month ago, I would have bragged about all the positives (if any) in Roxanne's day... but I've learned now that any niceties find me persecuted and oppressed all over again.

"She couldn't keep her eyes open after dinner (within three minutes of dinner)."

"Well, *you* need to keep her *awake*. That's your job."

But I don't *want* my job! I kept that inside my head, however.

Having had enough of the manipulations in Hell House, I told her, "I tried once, telling her 'You don't wanna be sleeping when Dolores comes down here,' but beyond that, I won't try further. I will not force her, as it can elicit more melodrama and attitude."

And the registered nurse tells me, consistently *inconsistent*, "Let her sleep then. What-the fuck-ever."

Dolores stayed longer than "her usual." She was rough and abrupt — abusive — with her mother. I need to no longer care; that's turning out to be a tough component of my personality from which to disconnect. An absence of caring and empathy is not who I am.

And in her typical pattern, Dolores interjects anything that she might think would "push my buttons," even in the smallest of ways. She told me there was snow in the forecast, and I told her that's not what Weather Canada says.

"Well, the *radio* says it's so." She was clearly baiting me to conflict, but I just let it go. We have above-zero temperatures projected all week, rain on Wednesday, and no snow forecasted all week. I'll take the Weather Canada disposition that's updated every half hour over the radio. I am a city girl, after all. The Farmer's Almanac won't help me navigate Kamloops' winter roadways!

It seemed Dolores was walking on eggshells with me, which was nice for a change. She could see I was exhausted.

"Should I stick around until 9 PM and turn Roxanne's lights out?" On the surface, most would consider that a polite query — but there was some foreshadowing in her presentation that I had witnessed many times. Dolores never offers *anything* out of the goodness of her heart; in fact, I'd like to see an ultrasound. I would bet there's no heart inside that cavity. Everything bears an underlying motive. I'll pass on even accepting a Kleenex from her, now.

"OH no, no worries — I've got that."

And here we go: before leaving, she told me the mattress had shifted. "Make sure you reposition that tomorrow." And with that, she turned and waddled with hunched shoulders out the door and back to her house up the hill.

JANUARY 15, 2017

Given my rather stringent boundaries of late, I have now removed all but the bare essentials of my personal effects. I've done this under the guise of placing things into storage — but in reality, I have secretly rented an inexpensive apartment in the city. Now, on my two days away from the client, I will stay in my personal accommodations overnight — and have Mattie there with me. He is *not* returning to Hell House

We will begin cleaning and unpacking next week and get everything set up. I am glad that I suffered through bringing my personal effects up here with me; to start over from nothing, still again, would have been impossible in the circumstances.

So now, I have a "10-strikes-you're-out" list. Every time I am confronted or bullied or slave-handled with more duties (which I refuse now), I add it to my list. The list started January 12 (the date I got the keys to my apartment) and already there are three strikes... but I can say affirmatively, that is a *significant* improvement. The women of Hell House have both smartened up and are walking on eggshells with me since I moved my belongings out. In that process, Dolores confronted me strongly and inappropriately in front of my son. She raised her voice and used a derogatory tone. My only response (twice) was, "Hey — no negativity, right?" This, before I turned and let her watch me walk away. This, I did as an example of decorum in conflict for my son. Inside my mind, I enjoyed the fantasy of leaving my handprint on her fact — but of course, that has never been my personality or response.

She ultimately walked away, but not before putting Mattie into tears over the completely unwarranted conflict. But, in hindsight, I believe *she* felt it was warranted because I showed I *am not trapped*, and *I will not kowtow and be controlled.*

Poor Mattie. I'm so grateful he is saddened these days rather than angered. None of us need to see anger and aggression from a 270–pound, 6-foot three-inch 38-year-old young man with a history of martial arts, boxing, and sports. No one here will ever be informed of his history — of gang involvement and extreme violence. Thank goodness, my young man has adopted the lessons of tolerance and gentility put his way since the traumatic brain injury, with commendable success through six of those 15 years. But no, it has not always been a "cakewalk."

Light at the end of the tunnel now — and it's not a train. I'm keeping my cool and proceeding with professional resolve. A return to the gym in two weeks is budgeted and strategized, and I hope to "*real employment*" in eight weeks, but need my head on straight first with some downtime. That is also all strategized on paper, with three different alternative solutions. Compulsive list-making for the win.

Goal: use *everything* as an opportunity to understand, grow, and expand. And commit the lessons learned to memory.

JANUARY 16, 2017

Roxanne was sleeping at 8:10, moaning in her sleep. When I awakened her, she said she was dreaming she was hunting — chasing a big bear!

"Have you ever had that dream before?"

"Nope!"

"Have you ever been hunting?"

"Nope!"

I speculate her dream has selected a big, aggressive bear as her daughter's "spirit animal." The fact that her subconscious mind is hunting the bear speaks volumes.

Having trouble zipping the same pink fleece top again this morning, which Roxanne insisted on wearing, despite an unrepaired zipper, I found myself irritated.

"This is the same top I put in the sewing room for Dolores to fix, when you told me to do that."

"Just take a bar of soap and run it over the zipper."

I told her no, I would not do that. Darleen could do that.

She snarled, "Give me a damn bar of soap and I'll do it."

"Then you'll need to tell me where I can find a bar of soap; there's no communication here, so I don't *know* where to find a bar of soap — and if I could not find a bar of soap, I certainly would not telephone Dolores to ask for one." She said nothing. My tone, my body language, and my facial expression surely showed I was not to be met with folly.

I absolutely refuse to allow one additional duty to be imposed upon me. I do more than any other caregiver here has done, and they keep asking for more. Those extras have concluded.

THANK G-D, tomorrow is my four-hour time off, and the two days after that are FULL DAYS off. I must admit I am rather excited about getting my place in order, getting a TV, and spending the night in my private space at last.

Instead of looking out her window this morning, Roxanne asks, "More snow?"

"Nope! No more snow — warmer temperatures — above zero... rain on Wednesday and no snow in the forecast all week."

In her grand capacity as a pseudo-meteorologist, she laughs cruelly, "Aren't YOU dreaming? You can *bet* there will be snow after that rain."

Having had enough, I submitted to my building anger.

"Yeah, I don't dream; my life is a fucked-up reality right now."

She retorted, with continuing cruelty in her voice, "Well, that's disgusting. You need to be more grateful."

"It certainly is disgusting." And with that, I turned and walked away, leaving her babbling alone.

Time to reposition Roxanne's mattress while she is having her post-breakfast tea and reading her book.

I stood behind the bed and pushed the mattress over. Dolores had instructed me to use the handles and pull the mattress from the other side.

Nice – she knows better, but thankfully, I do, too. Years of competitive bodybuilding taught me better than that. I speculate she was trying to set me up for another back injury. Being familiar with the stories of how these women refuse to begin CPR, wait to call an ambulance for injured or dying family, and so much more — this is completely within her *modus operandi* of tricks.

2:10 PM – I asked Roxanne if she was ready to go back for her afternoon nap at 2 PM and she said yes, but fiddled "OCD-style" for ten minutes. She folded a napkin on the table (then unfolded it, and folded it again), she sipped her tea, poured another half-cup, sipped again, and poured again, she spent about 40 seconds putting her bookmark into her book — and made eye contact with me twice while doing all this, so I know it was by design. I still said nothing; just waited for her to quit fiddling... Then she disengages the brakes on her wheelchair and starts pushing back into the cabinet behind her. I stopped her, half-picked her and the chair up and wheeled it around so as not to crash into the cabinet. Once I wheeled her down the hallway and assisted her to the commode, she says, "You better put your fan on cause I'm gonna stink up the place."

I tried to make light of a somber/heavy mood and said, "Well, good to know those prunes are doing their job."

She was there for an extended time on the commode. After 15 minutes, I returned to find her fiddling with toilet paper on her leg. She was smearing feces all over her thigh — like she was in art class! WTF? I stood there secretly around the corner in disbelief and watched her take a clean piece of toilet paper, trying to rub away the feces she had gotten on her panties. I asked if she was ready, from outside her room (she does not know I have been watching from a meager distance; I was able to view exactly what she was doing from the reflection in her bedroom window, opposite).

"I'm trying to clean this off – I don't know how it got there."

"You won't be able to clean that off your panties, Roxanne; we'll put a new pair on you."

Fine. I removed her trousers and her panties and provided a clean pair. She asked me to clean her thigh.

"No, you can do that — but I will get you a couple of warm, wet washcloths." I handed her two wet washcloths.

"I don't know how that got there. I didn't do it. It's your job to clean up my shit."

"Roxanne, *of course,* you did it — unless you are trying to tell me we have a mischievous ghost on board here. If that's what you think, just take that up with Dolores. But I stood there and *watched* you do it. I am NOT cleaning shit off the front of your thigh that you rubbed there on purpose. You clean it yourself."

She repeated, this time growling, "YOU do it."

"Nope — but I will get you dressed after you clean yourself up."

She cleaned her leg, handed me the two soiled washcloths, and I gave her a third.

"Make sure I got my backside clean," and she lifted one leg to show me her naked crotch!

"I will clean you off *after* you stand up, as per our usual."

She mumbled something else, and I told her I could not hear her. "What was that again?"

She motioned for me to move closer. When I leaned forward, within about 8 inches of her head, she gave me an uppercut with her left fist and hit me square in my right eye!

"Bet ya never sat *THAT* one coming," she snarled with a look that said she was proud of herself. I left the room, washed my face with cold water, and let her sit there, pondering her predicament.

Already, a black eye was surfacing. Lovely. I wondered if I still had any cover stick in my personal effects here. I was going to need to hide this from Mattie.

She stood, and I took another fresh, wet, and warm cloth, cleaned her backside, then pulled up her trousers. She then told me there was no pee-pad there and instructed me to put one on.

"NO, that is *your job* – YOU put the pad on. Those were Dolores' instructions, and that's the way we've done things for weeks. We are not changing things now." I watched as she sat back down on the commode and installed her pad, as she does every single day. She stood up again, and I pulled up her underwear and her trousers. I watched her climb into bed, and once there, handed her the book, pulled up her covers, confirmed her water was there on the nightstand, and told her, "I'll be back at dinner time."

JANUARY 16, 2017

Monday is my "almost Friday," as Tuesday brings me four hours of freedom while my client has a health-authority employee come in to bathe her... A week from tomorrow, those four hours will be spent at the gym for me — MY time, wholly and solely for me.

Then Wednesday and Thursday are my days off; this week to clean and complete the last transfer of my personal effects to my "secret apartment." Mattie will help with all that, and no matter how tiring it will invariably be, it's great bonding time for us both! Cable and Wi-Fi will be installed on Thursday morning, and my new temporary home will be complete!

As for my "10 Strikes I'm Out" list with this position, they've got five left. Five misdemeanors since January 12th (only four days), but a couple of weeks ago, before I engaged very firm boundaries, we were totaling over ten per day (all recorded in writing, lest I forget or my memory glosses over it to seem less horrific & invasive than it was).

ELDER ABUSE

C ountdown: nine days to liberty. It's January 22, 2017.

Roxanne rang her bell at 7:30 this morning, so my juice outlay, porridge, and wood stove fire duties were interrupted. On bringing her into the kitchen, after tending to her redressing after her morning pee, the first words catapulting strongly from her mouth were, "Can I have my pills?"

It pissed me off, so I snapped... "You woke up early, so your pills are coming, your breakfast is coming, your tea is coming."

Never giving up on how she can be her most-commanding bully, she snaps, "Are you even *going to* make a fire today?"

I remained kind — one snap was enough. "I was *making* the fire and had it started when you rang early. After I give you breakfast, I will start the fire." I added, before she could judge and criticize further, that I had let the dog out three times already, "And *today*, I will not be Sophie's designated servant every 15 minutes."

She whimpered, "I'm sorry." At least she is cognizant of me having had enough. I suppose there is some pity to be had for her; she is so miserable, so trapped, with no independence or autonomy remaining — and she, too, is bullied and degraded daily. The dysfunctional codependence between Roxanne and her overbearing daughter was undeniable.

I mentioned, "I think Dolores mistakenly brought us the wrong carton of eggs."
"Why?"

"There were only six in the carton and they were all broken. But, you know I waste nothing here, so I boiled three, and I ate three, so the eggs are still okay."

"So, call Dolores and tell her we need more eggs down here."

"NO, I am trying to avoid communications with Dolores because if she is in a bad mood, that will ruin *my* mood for the day."

She said *she* would call her, so I dialed the number for her and handed her the phone. In a sweet voice, she let her daughter know we needed more eggs — but carefully added, "There's no rush." There's the proof in the pudding again: Roxanne dreads a ruined day because of Dolores' mood swings as much as I do. At least, I can (and will) leave. Roxanne only has hope of a placement with Gemstone.

After Dolores came down with eggs and some more muffins, she left. She was not in an unpleasant mood — merely in her normal state of disgruntled bitchiness. While she was still here, Roxanne told her, "I think we should change my sheets every two weeks; we're using too much hydro and water and costing money we don't need to be spending with that. I don't go anywhere and the sheets aren't dirty every week."

Without even a moment's hesitation, Dolores snapped, "Don't you go there with me! If you want to change your sheets every two weeks, instead of every week, then you are going to have to sleep on the *other side of the bed* for a week. DON'T GO THERE."

Roxanne meekly replied, "But I can't *move* over to the other side of the bed."

Dolores' *very strong and very loud* response was, "Whose problem is that? You make it *mine* if you change the rules. SO, we change the sheets once a week; we've been doing that FORever and we're not making changes now — or *ever*."

Wow. Elder abuse — but not my circus, not my monkeys.

JANUARY 22, 2017

Turning my focus concertedly back to tight nutrition, structured weight training, and regular cardio seems to be a good plan. I have allowed some serious stressors to get the better of me lately and have been slacking — mostly because of an inability to get to the gym (yes, being confined 24 hours out of five consecutive days prevents one from attending a gym). I have held true in daily stretching lately, and have been using my gallon jugs of water for some rudimentary weight training at home, but I am *so* ready to get back into some disciplined residual hard-core workouts again.

My freedom is only a few days away now and I am turning my focus away from the stress to APPRECIATE EVERYTHING THAT I DO HAVE. Yeah, all caps on that one — I figure I need to *shout it* to myself!

I think we'd all agree that life is hard. And indeed, for whatever reasons or just plain unfortunate circumstances, it *is* harder for some than it is for others... Some of that reflects poor decision-making, and some of it is because of uncontrollable downturns in health...

There's invariably an optimal way to approach the hard times, but over 62 years, I have learned that taking the *easier* route is almost never the better path.

We should never short-circuit our path to change, advancement, or goals achieved. And in the same context, we should never bypass opportunities to exit situations that cause us harm. It's a call to research, make a list, chart out and weigh the pros and cons of potential decisions, and make educated maneuvers.

Today, my 'Lucky Seven' charting looks like this:

1. List the scenario(s) to change
2. Why the change is needed
3. What's on me in what went wrong?
4. What's in other circumstances with what went wrong?
5. Option 1 with pros & cons, what COULD interrupt the process, and how to rectify it
6. Option 2 with pros & cons, what COULD interrupt the process, and how to rectify it
7. DECISION: THE RIGHT ROAD

THE RIGHT ROAD, *not the easier road.*

Tonight's Menu
- Pork chops with sauerkraut & pineapple (a German recipe)
- Roasted red potatoes
- Cabbage with sauteed mushrooms
- Cornbread

And for *me?* Chicken breast & asparagus (my final meal of the day is always carb-free — it's back to a little gentle diet-down now)!

When I presented the dinner to Roxanne, she looked at me as though to express, "WTF now?", but said nothing. She proceeded to pick apart everything on her plate, which I ignored. After about 15 minutes of that, she finally ate every speck of food served. As I was washing some dishes while she finished her meal, I actually observed her using her finger to get all the sauce off the plate.

"Me thinks thou doth protest too much."

I am confident it is her conditioned response now — to seek conflict in any small capacity. But since I refused to take the bait, my position being that she is an adult — if she doesn't want to eat, I can give her some pudding — she ate her dinner, and clearly enjoyed it all.

And just like that, a memory from my distant past traveled up to the forefront of my mind! In my first marriage, a bad decision opted at the tender age of 17, I prepared meals for which my then-husband never expressed gratitude. One night, I asked if he liked the pot roast meal I'd prepared. Just now, I heard his grating voice inside my mind: "I'm eating it, aren't I?"

Awww, my Mattie... Just got another sweet email from him now, and *these* are the moments that make everything worthwhile! He continues to be my "why", and it's not lost on me, it's more ways than one. My why for continuing, my why for persevering — and right now, in wanting and needing to be closer to him, to protect him, my why for suffering.

> "CHURCH WAS AWESOME!! I'M LOVED, LIKE, TRULY, BY THE PEEPS THERE!! WE HAVE PRAYED 4 U TOO! I LOVE U, AND LOOKING 4WERD 2 SEEING U!! ML"

The "ML" in his sign-off translates to mean "my love." Oh my; he keeps forgetting that's not the most appropriate way to address your mother... but he means oh so well!

8:56 PM
After Dolores left, having given Roxanne another lecture for not knowing what day of the week it was... and commanding her to look at her calendar, Roxanne asked me who the advertiser was for the calendar on the wall.... I told her it was a funeral home. She looked down at her hands, then chuckled.

I told her I would stop at the dollar store tomorrow on my time off and see if I could find her a HAPPY calendar.

WOW, still again. If it's not games with me, it's games with each other.

Roxanne has wet her pants two out of three times going to pee today. I was very careful to pull her trousers and underpants ALL the way down to her ankles, so I have yet to figure out how she does this. I got frustrated with her tonight (5 PM) and slipped and said, "Well, it doesn't matter, I will not be here much longer, anyway." Whoops! Anger and frustration trigger my impulsivity.

She asked, "Why?"

"Why do you think?" Then I promptly corrected my hasty comment and told her, "Thank G-D, I have two days off coming."

To this, sharp as a tack — a complete absence of dementia — she meekly replied, "And four hours."

I said, "Yes, it's a good warm-up"... and dropped the subject.

JANUARY 23, 2017
Observation: insecure and difficult individuals all-too-often sport a "know it all" attitude. They also refuse to converse about anything other than that with which they are familiar. Introduce a topic new to them, especially if you have the expertise and know what you're talking about? Well, you either see the subject changed, or you see the bitter retorts to fly, *or* they walk away, because (1) they have no interest — but more than that, (2) they have no capacity to understand and have no interest in learning.

Case in point, in my short-lived employment scenario with Hell House, Roxanne's daughter snapped at me last night (criticizing the trouble I'd gone to in preparing an enjoyable meal for her mother). Earlier, when I said I was preparing a mango salsa, she told me, "Be sure to give her some crackers with that because last time she didn't know how to eat it." I mentioned last time was guacamole with avocados (and fresh veggies provided for dipping), and she retorted "Avocado - Mango — all the same."

'Ya just can't make this stuff up or predict what's coming next! But one *can* predict a countdown to freedom!

EXCELLENCE is not an act — but (rather) a habit.

Helping my son through brain injury over the last 15 years has taught me so much. One of the most invaluable practices for *any* brain-injury survivor is to develop a structure in daily living... to condition oneself to a litany of "little things" — seemingly inconsequential practices (such as putting things back in the same place consistently, and in the same manner, starting the day by making the bed before anything else, redirecting negative thoughts to what makes you happy, then to what you're grateful to have in your life)...

From this, I have learned that we *all* suffer certain levels of disability, despite all our high-functioning lifestyles, accelerated pace, and what we *think* to be incessant multitasking. No one multi-tasks proficiently; they only think they are accomplishing more — but they are sacrificing something from each level of accomplishment, to contribute in a lesser capacity to another accomplishment. Sorry, I deter.

Excellence in spirit is reinforced by learning from each negative and hurtful experience (and believe me, I'm still having those lessons handed to me on a tarnished platter). Just a few examples include:

- ALWAYS choosing the road of integrity as its foundation rather than the sometimes overwhelming desire for vindication or justice
- ALWAYS speaking up for what is right, but consistently communicating with decorum
- ALWAYS being the kinder response, no matter what they throw in your face

Do I have my negative and vindictive thoughts? Oh, hell yes... Do I act on them? Seldom, and if I do, it is with advance legal consult — and never with violence or illegality... But when I experience these I work diligently to redirect my thinking (as I have taught my son to do) to a more positive mindset, to a happier place — and to EVER BE COGNIZANT that bad times are invariably temporary. In Mattie's words, "This too shall pass, like gas."

Take the lesson and run with it. We *are* what we repeatedly do... May we all choose to be the better person. May *I ever choose to be a better human.* Most days, a lot of extra effort is required at Hell House and I am losing my motivation to continue the endurance contest.

> "We are what we repeatedly do. Excellence, then, is not an act, but a habit."   ~Aristotle

Ahhh, still another tale from "the dark side" of my last days with Hell House.

Despite all the horrors (and they are very real, though I have not elaborated on all), I feel pity for Roxanne, despite her mean-spirited, manipulative, and sometimes violent propensities. While I am still here, I am trying to teach her to keep in touch with what day of the week it is (as her days lived from the confinement of a wheelchair blend into one mushy blob). Two days ago, we asked her daughter to provide a wall calendar.

Before I wheeled Roxanne back to retire for the evening tonight, Roxanne glanced at the funeral home calendar again. It clearly bothered her deeply, and I am confident that in the same situation, I would be distressed, as well. She merely said, "Well, I guess she's shopping. I sure don't need to see that, but she'll keep behaving this way. Guess she would not help me any more than she helped... no, I'd better not go there. We're all gonna die."

Is it me, being over-reactive and over-sensitive to my empathy at the forefront — or is this *just wrong?* I submit it is the latter.

I have four hours off tomorrow, while the bath girl is here, and I will be picking up a puppy calendar at the store for her. The funeral home calendar will become celebrated kindling in very short order, and should Dolores challenge me on the change, I am up to the challenge. I am as good as gone now. Bring it, troll.

COUNTDOWN TO ESCAPE

W hen you have a deadline for a goal, you count the days... or the hours (16 8)... or you do your countdown in minutes, as I do (10,080 and lessening)! And thankfully, Wednesday and Thursday are days off, to be spent with my son and final-preparing my little apartment for entry.

I feel there's a wee light at the end of the tunnel now, seven days to freedom, sanity and to practice the lessons I've learned through this traumatizing experience (traumatizing: defined as "subject to lasting shock because of an emotionally disturbing experience or physical injury." I have both categories covered — emotional disturbance and physical injury).

The morning went reasonably well with Roxanne. I vacuumed and mopped floors, cleaned both bathrooms, did a load of laundry, got the fire started, gave her breakfast and meds, and pre-made her lunch for the bath girl to serve (labeling that in the fridge, in case one of the Bath Girls devoid of common sense arrives today), emptied all garbage, and brought in two more buckets of wood (so Dolores doesn't have to do any of that on Wednesday and Thursday when I am off).

BUT, I find my patience is dissipating the closer I get to my finalization date. Sometimes, I think stretching out my presence here just one more week — and the $200 would come in very handy. Or if I could withstand two more weeks, $400 would make a significant improvement to my budget. I will play it by ear. If more bullshit and attitude transpires, I will follow my plan to leave without notice, and just leave a note on Wednesday morning, February 1st. If these two women have any semblance of respect over the next five days, I will *consider* telling them I am leaving once I have my payroll in hand. I will offer to stay one week, on their agreement to pay me after one week — and I will consider staying the extra week (again on the same agreement) if there are no disrespectful or negative commentaries. I cannot possibly speculate what will transpire.

It is frustrating and peculiar for me to plan life, based on $200-$400. There was a time, and not so long ago, I earned that in one day.

I returned after my four hours off. I'd been in the trailer 15 minutes (sitting at my computer) when Roxanne called out in a "grating" tone, "Ta-*reesa*."

TERESA? More games — who the frack is Teresa? And what is her purpose with this? Does she *want* me to leave? Or does she *think I won't?* This one is well beyond my ability to comprehend. It denies reasoning. Medical experts have affirmed no diagnosis of dementia.

I went to her room and asked what she needed. She asked me to bring her Robert's telephone number. I brought her the book I'd made for her and looked it up, and recited the number for her.

After she finished her call, I took her folded laundry into her room to put away. In one of her moods still, she snarled, "What are you doing?"

I told her I was putting away her laundry. I added, with a purposeful kindness in my voice, "You know — I have been here *nine* weeks, and you still don't know my name."

She growled, "Hmph! I called you Teresa, and you came! So, whatever works! Bet if I call you Cynthia, you'd come to that, too."

"My name is not Teresa, never has been, and for nine weeks, no one named Teresa has even visited. It is disrespectful that you do not remember the name of someone who has helped you so much for nine weeks — a bit like a slave mentality that I am your servant, and my name is insignificant."

Knowing full well what she had done, she snarled, "Well, I pay you; I can call you whatever the fuck I want to call you and if I call you Teresa and you come, I don't see the problem with that. You need to just put up and shut up! Are those not words you like? Just do your job and quit bitching, Cynthia."

"Roxanne, I am truly at my wit's end here — and I really won't take any more disrespect in this house." She said nothing. I turned and walked away. I exited the trailer and walked up the property to have a chat with Dave, Dolores' husband (and the only amicable, rational person on the property). Distressed, I told him my last day would be Tuesday; he said he could have never expected me to last as long as I did. Dave shared an extensive and morbidly fascinating history of the family. Roxanne was a problem *long* before the stroke left her disabled, that her first husband left her because she was "a controlling bitch." Dave shared he had almost left Dolores because of Roxanne and the way Dolores clings to and craves her control of all this. He also told me that Robert, the son, wanted nothing to do with the mother, adding that he only performed his due diligence in coming up here to visit three times per year.

When Dolores returned with groceries at 7:45, I told her quietly and calmly, privately in the kitchen, that Tuesday would be my final day... that I would work through the day and leave (as I always do on my day off) Wednesday morning — just this time I would not be returning.

She took it well, but of course, had to render an insult, being the expert in gaslighting that she was: "Most people give two weeks' notice."

"Ahh, you've never had a caregiver here that gave you two weeks' notice — remember? And Dolores — this is not a professional position. If it *were* a professional position, I've been here less than 90 days — and in that timeframe, under BC employment law, no notice is required — either by an employer or by an employee leaving. You seem to conveniently forget that I worked in personal injury law, employment law, and municipal law for almost 40 years – and I will return to it in the city."

She continued with insult, "You're just too emotionally fragile for this job, anyway." I laughed, "Nah, there was so much more than that and I have a few recorded conversations to prove it," adding "But, it stands — I am gone after Tuesday."

"Well, just don't go away mad!" It was apparent my resignation held no surprise for her, and she was well aware of the requirements for notice vacating a position such as this. I suppose she, like her husband, was surprised I had endured for as long as I had. For her, however, it became a contest of the wills — to see how far she could push and how much I would endure.

I said I was not mad — just tired. She asked what I would do, and I told her I would cash in one RRSP and return to work in legal. She seemed bewildered by that information, and I found it a bit sadly hilarious that she could think this would be some glorious career position for me.

Whatever. I feel better now that my decision is final and now and openly disclosed; I don't like secrets or deception. There will be no extension for another week, and certainly not another two weeks.

JANUARY 25, 2017

Got another cram-filled carload of my personal effects off to the little apartment, after getting preparations out of the way for Dolores' care of her mother. Of course, nothing will be acknowledged. There will be no gratitude or appreciation — but I am almost out of here. After dropping the contents of my car off at the apartment, I picked up Mattie for a breakfast outing. Bless him, he wants to be with me no matter what I am doing. He cannot help with the apartment organization, however, and I invariably worry about his boredom, as a bored Mattie finds trouble. I cannot let him smoke outside without overseeing him, as the neighborhood is not conducive to crime-free living and he has already tried to seek marijuana — telling me that the woman downstairs smokes weed and one apartment across the parking lot is a dealer's apartment. Yikes, it took him all of one hour here to figure that out. I see him as childlike in so many ways, and I want to reach a point of trust with him — but I also keep "forgetting" that he is sly, he can strategize and be patient enough to plan and when prepared (or dissociated), to strike without warning. Certainly, he can snuff out marijuana and those who use it better than a K9 unit.

I have not placed my knives in the kitchen drawers here... I keep going in and out of concern/fear of Matt and those knives. Each time I let my guard down, there is some little behavior from him — something in his eyes that he quickly corrected with "I love you SO MUCH, Mom" and hugs that keep my intuition on alert. It has become apparent that he is *cognizant* that his altered psyche is showing through. But, of course, I know him better than he knows himself. In fact, that is another one of his catchphrases, repeated frequently.

He seems so grateful that I am back in Kamloops for him, but as he becomes more and more unhappy with group home management, he is also creating more and more problems there. This repeat pattern concerns me deeply. But what am I to do? My rescuing him is enabling on the one hand, but with the TBI, I want to keep him out of institutionalization or jail. I want to keep him off the streets; I want to keep him alive. He might live semi-independently one day. I still have some hope. He is intelligent, and he *is* capable — but he is a manipulator and will handle anyone to do his bidding, including me. It's another reason he could so readily identify the bullying and manipulation in Hell House, despite about 98 percent of it having been hidden from him.

I feel very trapped in my deep love for him. I feel very trapped here in Kamloops, too.

JANUARY 26, 2017
It was a whirlwind of two days off from the home care position. I accomplished a lot, shopping and purchasing minimal supplies to complete a few repairs, which the manager said would be up to me to perform. The place was filthy, too, but beggars can't be choosers. When I asked if the radiators would be cleaned inside, he laughed! There are almost no rental vacancies in Kamloops presently, and what is available is devoid of niceties.

At least I am adept at cleaning, and the place is smelling like lemon juice now!

ALSO, I have found myself "less than lousy" at repairing drawers, floor moldings, and cabinets. I've learned by trial & error, but since management has no interest in making the repairs, if I want it done, it's up to me. I will be fully vacated in less than a week from now. Onward and upward!

JANUARY 27, 2017
Whew — busy two days off. It was so enjoyable to be away from Hell House. I returned around 3:30. Dolores was not there, so I had a shower and then crawled into bed. I had oatmeal cookies for dinner. As I did not want to see either of the Hell House power mongers, I kept to myself.

Matthew is worried that Dolores is going to play with my pay, or downright refuse to pay me. Bless him, no matter the deficits, sometimes his mind is sharp; it is what continues to have me holding hope, and I truly pray it is not the variety of hope that makes me see what I want to see. After all, how do we know the difference? How can others even accurately assess that?

Ahh, again, I deter... I don't think Dolores will withhold or deny my pay, but if she does, I do not know what my recourse would or could be. All I can do is maintain composure, remain professional, complete the bare-minimum duties entailed with this position and take one day at a time.

It was an excellent decision to have extended no consideration to these people above and beyond Tuesday.

Dolores rolled in around 10:50 AM with bitchy body language and verbal tone, but I still offered a "GOOD morning!" She uttered "morning" under her breath, but within a minute, she altered her tone — seeming to reconsider that she should zip a lip. Ultimately, she left after only about five minutes, asking Roxanne (then me) if we needed anything from town. "Nothing for now — but thanks! Have an awesome day" I'm confident that irritates her; when one is as consistently miserable and enjoys her expertise in bitchery, an excess of positivity can just exacerbate the folly further. I will assuage my tolerance levels soon!

I escorted Roxanne to her room for a nap (and pee) at 2 PM. She started peeing before I could even get her trousers down and her face reflected forced urination; she had done that on purpose, still again. Nice to see she has a going-away present for me. But Karma is ever-observant and though we don't always get to see Lady Karma work her magic, I have to admit it slightly elated me to see her sit down and pinch her legs on the toilet seat. She shrieked, "OUCH!" in the most negative of tones, and glared at me as though I had prearranged the "bite," but I did not buy into it. Instead, I just walked into the bathroom calmly to raise the toilet seat, prepared to deposit her urine once she was done. Now, I merely do my job, nothing more, and nothing less — with polite impartiality.

When Dolores visited tonight (around 7:40), she was cordial — not friendly, but polite. She seemed annoyed by her mother's existence. Eileen, the other daughter, phoned — Dolores answered the telephone and was flippant to her. She left while Roxanne was engaged in a conversation with Eileen. I could hear Roxanne say, "I can't really talk right now. I don't know *what* they're going to do."

When I last spoke with Dave, Dolores' husband, he had shared that no live-in homemaker/caregiver had lasted as long as I had, adding that most left in the first week, and one had even left after only three hours! He said I was the only one that could cook, but he also told me that no amount of caring or quality work ethic would ever be enough for his wife or her mother. "Their only joy comes from complaining, demanding, and seeing others miserable. Nothing is ever enough for these two."

At 7:57, I prepared to take Roxanne to her bedroom; she tallied long before disengaging the brake from her wheelchair, fiddling with the laptop (suddenly it was of interest, although she had been reading a book seconds earlier), fiddling with napkins on the table, fiddling with her teacup... Once back in her room, she took five full minutes before making any effort to transition from the wheelchair and onto the commode... checking the seat first. "Last time, you had that seat rigged to bite me in the ass." I saw that same "forced" look on her face and realized she was trying to pee on me again, but I got her trousers down before she could "perform." After all, I've always been competitive. I win on this one tonight!

Roxanne took more than the usual time to push herself over in the bed. My empathy has expired, however. I emptied her garbage and her commode and did my end-of-night chores in her bedroom while she pretended to struggle. It is the first time I have done that, but it will be my practice over these last four days and nights. She made more exaggerated dramatic "ouch" commentaries with the pulling of the blankets over her feet...

I came here to HELP — wanting to make her life more enjoyable with a clean house, making her a phone book, a high-quality array of meals... but alas, nothing was ever good enough. I was her slave; no more, no less.

THREE MORE SLEEPS, and thank G-D for sleeping pills to get me over the hump with it all.

Don't let hindsight be 20-20. Learn to trust and heed your intuition. That's not just my "message to self" — it's to anyone reading this far.

Case in point, in hindsight, from the time I interviewed for the "caregiving position," I knew something wasn't quite right — but I wanted to change my career and locate myself closer to my son *so* desperately, I did not heed the warning signs. This is what happens when we find ourselves making rash decisions in response to a crisis.

By week two, I knew something at Hell House was very wrong... toxic, twisted, negative... but I thought perhaps I was over-reacting... thought I could persevere and make positive change for the two women on this property. I thought I could make a difference — be the hero. Persevere, this too shall pass... everything's gonna be alright. Alas, again in hindsight, I was dreadfully ignoring my intuition.

Nine weeks in — and out permanently at week ten (in a few short days), my journal clarifies the shocking reality of what has transpired here, along with qualified input from professionals (including two RCMP and one lawyer) and a handful of trusted friends; nothing was an over-reaction on my part at any material time.

Life is absolutely too short to waste a moment failing to trust what our experience has taught us. After all, doing the same things simply delivers the same results. If we don't learn from the opportunities presented, we get the lesson again.

DISRESPECT BY ANY OTHER NAME

T oday marks my final Saturday at Hell House. It's January 28, 2017. KINDNESS WINS, in the end. Two events today altered my perception of the future and how our karma renders lessons (good and bad, according to our chosen actions).

This morning, I saw Roxanne struggling with irritation in her right eye. I asked gently if she wanted some eye drops in there. She looked at me in amazement and said, "Why would you do that for me?" I told her, "Roxanne, I don't *hate* you. I've always been here to help you." With that, I put some solution in her eyes. Of course, there was no reciprocal thank you, but her mood improved right away; that's all that matters — and the FACT she had a lesson to ponder (and I felt like the better person).

Dolores' husband (Dave) stopped by with a huge grin on his face! I had gifted him Mattie's former $1,500 Danier leather jacket, as Mattie could not pull it shut for a long time. I initially gave it to Dolores and received no gratitude. Typical — and I shame myself for even thinking a random act of kindness would produce any thanks. But today, Dave sported a professionally tailored leather jacket that looked brand new! He was so proud and even offered to give me money for the jacket. I refused, saying was a gift from our hearts and nothing changed that, but knowing he could use it and was happy with it was one of the best things in our new year. He gave me a hug and thanked me three or four more times before leaving! Both Mattie and I have, at all material times, adored and respected this gentleman.

I believe we must ALWAYS choose the kinder path, the path of integrity — if it is even remotely humanly possible. I equally believe there is a time and a place appropriate for an emphatic response. TODAY, KINDNESS WINS!

For tonight's dinner, I started the plate with a dill sauce, just a little for minor flavor & the pretty lime-green color... Then in the center of the plate, brown rice with green peas, shaped with a two-inch bowl, to make it pretty on top of the dill sauce... Then, lobster tails on top of that, with some coconut oil, sea salt & lemon juice drizzled over the top. Side veggies included steamed asparagus and glazed carrots (I wanted to see if the carrots were eaten this time).

Well, the *dog* absolutely went crazy wanting some, and I thoroughly enjoyed mine, but Roxanne took one look at the presentation and grunted. She then stirred it all together and ate half, including the carrots!

This household is so ludicrous and toxic, that I just have to laugh! Three more sleeps and I'm out!

As Mattie would say, "Who's counting? I AM!"

JANUARY 29, 2017
"Drrring... drrring... drrring." The phone rang at 7:25 AM. I'd forgotten how shrill a ring those older landlines projected! But few could sleep through that — so I suppose it's a good thing in this household.

While I was completing all preliminaries for Roxanne's wake-up, she rings her bell. I already had the meds out and the juices out, getting ready to pour the coffee and put the porridge in the microwave. I went back, said good morning, and was told, "I need to go to the toilet in the worst way." Fine. As I *carefully and gently* removed her left night sock, I got the MEGA-DRAMATIC "Ouch."

WHATever... guess it's just gonna be that kind of day again. I waited for her to get up and scoot over so she could stand (I had to warn her if she tried from a mid-bed position, she would fall). I finally got her onto the commode and changed her clothes. She kept fiddling with a piece of Kleenex she had taken from the bed. Carefully, I tried to take it from her, so I could get her shirt off and put on a clean one, and she jerked it away from me. She was told to stop fiddling with the Kleenex and focus after I took it away from her — careful to do that *gently.* "I need to change your shirt and can't do that while you're fiddling with the Kleenex."

She was furious, not unlike a toddler being rescued from reaching for a toy too close to the top of a flight of stairs. But, it's too late: I no longer care about her emotional rhetoric. I handed her the hearing aide; she put it in. THEN, I gently asked, "Can you hear me?"

She mumbled, "Yeah, I'm not deaf."

I gently told her I am trying to help her and trying to get her clothes changed, as we do EVERY SINGLE MORNING. She said nothing, but finally complied and stopped "fighting me." Wonderful.

As I removed her slippers again, of course, I got the dramatic and exaggerated "ouch" response, despite my being very careful to be gentle with her. Balderdash! There's just no winning with this miserable woman. Finally, she got her pee on and I waited for her to stand, so I could pull up her trousers. She sat in the chair, disengaged the brakes, and pushed back with her feet.

WE NEVER EVER DO THINGS THAT WAY. I cannot imagine her purpose in pushing my buttons like this. Is it one last hurrah before I exit? I used my strength to prevent her from pushing back and pulled her shawl over her head, completing her dress-up for the morning. Then, I brushed her hair and wheeled her out and to the kitchen. I think she *forgot* to be dramatic on the rolling ride down the hallway.

While she ate her porridge and had her coffee and medications, I made a ground-chicken meatloaf for her dinner.

By 9 AM, I was *trying* to start a semblance of a congenial conversation with her, and told her I'd made a meatloaf... I had to repeat myself three times and asked if her hearing aid was not working again.

"No — I was reading my laptop and didn't want to talk to you."

I said fine, I would leave her to her laptop — and with that, she gave me a disgruntled "thank *YOU*," dismissing my servitude and presence.

I made one last effort to be kind, adding, "I made the meatloaf with ground chicken instead of ground beef — something different and a little healthier."

Her retort (just like her daughter would offer) was, "There's probably more fat in the chicken than in the beef."

Lovely — suddenly, she's a nutritional expert. That was enough, and I snapped, "ALRIGHT, there is NO pleasing you — NOTHING is ever enough. I am done with the polite conversational response in the face of adversity now. Two more sleeps and I am out. Winner, winner chicken dinner for me! *Nothing* is ever enough. I came in here to help you — to make your life a little better for whatever time I could, and I've constantly been met with resistance, disrespect, and abuse. You *assaulted me, Roxanne — for G-D's sake*. I am done."

With that, I turned and walked away. I was firm and *cold*, but I never raised my voice, never used profanity, and walked away with decorum. She said nothing... and put her head down for a minute.

It is abundantly clear that she is aware of what she is doing. I know she realizes she is intentionally cruel and disrespectful, and like her daughter, I *know* she enjoys making others around her feel threatened, miserable, insecure, and uncomfortable.

As per our typical protocols, I left her to her laptop and her book after removing her breakfast dishes, washing those and putting them away — and made her a fresh pot of tea.

By 11:14 AM, I heard Roxanne trying to wheel her wheelchair around in the kitchen, so I get up from my bedroom computer and asked her if she wanted to go back to the commode. She snarled, "YES, and I need to go FAST!"

I scold her gently, saying I cannot read her mind, adding she needs to let me know when she needs to go — that I am a mere eight feet away from her.

She has soiled herself with diarrhea. I changed her lower clothing and gave her three warm washcloths with which to wipe her legs. After that, I used a warm 4th cloth to wipe her down. She actually apologized. I told her I knew this was humiliating for her and I am sorry she had the experience.

BUT hey — back to reality: this is Hell House, after all. No good deed goes unpunished. Without hesitation, she demands to know what she had to eat that did this to her. I stated the only thing she had different yesterday was the cantaloupe, that I ate it and that Dolores and Dave ate it, and we were fine. Perhaps she had a wee "bug."

When I served her lunch, I omitted the high-fiber celery and gave her only cucumbers with the dressing she has had for 1.5 weeks — the same dressing she told Dolores she liked, the same dressing Dolores purchased a second time, last Tuesday.

She ate her pudding before the cucumbers, of course, and curtly asked what was in the bowl. I told her cucumbers, and that she did not need more fiber since celery was high in fiber.

"What's *on* it?" I told her it was the same dressing she had every day for almost two weeks now.

"And the same dressing I have picked off every time!"

I told her that was simply not true, "But hey, no worries; it can go to the trash!" I reminded her she had told Dolores she liked the dressing, and that was the reason they bought a second bottle. ALWAYS a complaint, ALWAYS negativity — and ALWAYS within seconds of me trying to be nice.

Reminder to self: no more niceties. Not one.

Two more sleeps.

When I have a deadline, I measure almost everything I do as in "lasts," LOL!

This morning, I baked the last meatloaf for Hell House and the last cake.

I also brought in more wood from outdoors for the last time — leaving a sufficient stack in the living room to last through Wednesday (being the better person, knowing it will go unappreciated and unacknowledged – but still the right thing to do).

LASTS, grand finales — all leading up to progress toward new FIRSTS!

JANUARY 30, 2017
7:10 AM

I awaken to no water in the trailer — no hot water, no cold water, and no ability to flush a toilet. I momentarily panic, wondering if I could *possibly* have failed to leave two faucets dripping. Not a chance — I've been focused and fastidious to leave two faucets dripping, as I have done (as instructed) over ten weeks here so the pipes would not freeze. I still expected Roxanne or her daughter seeking to blame me for this, but I placed a call to the main house. Thankfully, it was Dave who answered.

"Good morning, Dave; sorry to call so early, but we have no water down here." He's always so calm — says they'll sort it out and if I need a shower, to come up to the main house, no worries. He added they would bring down a couple of water jugs for washing dishes, making coffee, drinking, etc.

When I got Roxanne up, it was actually with a little amusement that I handed her a *cold* wet cloth to wash her face. I let her touch it first and saw the anger in her eyes, and I smiled, and said, "We have no water this morning!"

As predicted, I was greeted with intense and instant negativity, as though this was *her* property (it is not)! "WELL GREAT – this happens every damn year, this time of year. They'll have to get on that right away," she growls...

Well, I am privy to a little *insider information* on this count. Last Tuesday, when I was enlightened by Dave about the longstanding scenario here, he told me, "I've had more than enough of this shit. Roxanne freeloads off our land. Dolores and I bought this with no contribution from anyone else, and that includes that bitch down there in the trailer."

With a slightly peppy voice, I told her, "Ahhh, they have a breakfast outing; they will go to that and come back later in the day."

Instantly, she gave a SHARP know-it-all retort and said, "NOPE! They'll cancel that breakfast!" Proof, once again, that she absolutely *enjoys* the misery of others. But I had to admit that it seemed to be contagious; I was a little ashamed to admit that I was taking pleasure in the misery of these two women.

As she was trudging herself up upright from her bed, she commanded me to go behind the bed for a dropped Kleenex box. I refused, saying, "There's toilet paper over here. You can use that, and I will retrieve the Kleenex box later. You don't stand to mount the toilet with Kleenex in your hands, remember?" She said nothing, as she has played that game with me every morning for the past week.

When Dave & Dolores came down with water, they said they would be back, as they were going to breakfast! I commended them for that and added a cheery, "Enjoy!" Dave gave a sly smile and Dolores gave a "Whatever." Once they were out the door, I mockingly said to Roxanne (gently but with a slightly cocky smile), "TOLD 'ya they would go to breakfast!" She was as stunned as she was enraged. I'm feeling rather sanctimonious on this my last day of servitude!

I have pre-made enough porridge that Dolores has enough for three more mornings. That will be another nicety to her I leave behind, as a professional. Always be the better person. That's a fairly low bar around here, as there's so little in the way of respect and nicety.

I also brought in three more buckets of wood, as it is disappearing fast with the cold weather (minus 27 this morning) and the outdoor woodpile is seriously diminishing. Dolores also has not brought kindling down for days... I gathered some scraps off the ground, which will enable me to start the stove tomorrow morning, but after that, she is on her own for Wednesday. I do suspect that all this sudden inattention to regular duties was purposeful, to make my last days and hours here more work. Realizing that, however, simply made me want to be "the better person." No longer my circus, no longer my monkeys, thank G-D.

As for food in the fridge, Tuesday night I am going to remove the package of boneless/skinless chicken breasts.

The entirety of the fish supply has been cooked and will be eaten today and tomorrow. Meatloaf for Roxanne through tomorrow (since it is her favorite and easy for her to cut and chew), along with peas with corn, can supplement that, together with some of the white asparagus Roxanne had requested.

Today, there will be no changing of bed linens or sweeping of floors (I did that yesterday, in plain view of Roxanne). It takes considerable effort to get me to this position, but I no longer care. I now do what every other caregiver here has done — the minimum. And I will soon leave and never return. On Tuesday, after Roxanne is down for bed (9 PM), I will load my computer, monitor, and final clothing into the car. I will make my grand final exit around 9:30 PM. It will be a slow and precarious drive with my night-blindness, but I do not want to remain here another night.

The water came back on around 11:30 AM. Without delay, I phoned Dolores to let her know. I found her to be in the happiest mood I'd ever heard from her. Turns out, she and Dave had brunch with friends at the casino and played a few games there, and she had never done that before! It's about time she had some fun with her husband, away from her miserable, thankless and bitter mother.

She said Dave triggered the pump on the Well reservoir, and water started flowing again; Roxanne's dysfunctional toilet ran all the water out. I told her jiggling the handle no longer worked, nor did the manipulation of the inside apparatus in the tank, but was ignored for the full ten weeks I'd been here. There have been so many situations to dance around and endure here. She told me just to shut off the valve until such time I needed to flush the toilet. I did.

Roxanne seemed annoyed that I was having such a pleasant conversation with Dolores, so I didn't share the news with her right away. I returned about 15 minutes later and matter-of-factly told her we had water again. She asked, negatively, if Dave hooked water up to his house and I replied, "No, her toilet had not been working properly for a long time and ran all the water out last night."

She snapped, "Well, I don't use that toilet."

Now, no longer inclined to be the better person, I gave a smart-ass, cynical cackle and said, "Your pee and shit is *all* that goes into that toilet. Stop it!" I recognize I had responded inappropriately, but for the first time in my life, I was talking back. I no longer cared. More proof, it is time for me to go — and leave the two women of Hell House to their own indiscretions and competitive cruelty.

She grunts, "Well, I don't *see* it."

Almost enjoying the ludicrous game now, I snapped back, "Well, that doesn't mean it doesn't exist, does it? If a tree falls in the forest and no one is there, does it still make a sound? Stop it!" I walked away to my room to ignore her still again.

As ever, she can do no wrong. Everything is someone else's fault; she takes zero ownership or responsibility and only belittles and judges those around her. But I'll give her this: she is an expert in gaslighting and she perseveres!

Can I find a blessing in the pissy mix? THANK G-D — only one more sleep. Not much more can go wrong with only one more sleep in the countdown.

And perhaps it is time to pray that G-D takes me home promptly if I *ever* transform into such a miserable, entitled, and ungrateful creature as these women of Hell House.

EXIT, STAGE LEFT

D EAR HEAVENS: 5:20 PM — Roxanne finished her dinner, and her post-dinner dessert (rice pudding)... I noticed she had already taken her meds (typically taken around 7:30). I queried it and she said, with a curt and confrontational tone, "They fell into my pudding!" Of course, they did. Those pills animated. I'm just sorry I missed the performance. Those meds were positioned to her far right, on top of a Tupperware container... the pudding was positioned to her far left, about 18 inches away. She has a bad right arm... so??

I simply mocked her tone, "Well, THAT's a good one."

Dolores rolled in around 7:15. I dutifully took Roxanne's bloodwork (early). Dolores asked her mother how everything was today and she said "Fine." I opted to not share what a bitter and uncooperative idiot the woman had been. That's nothing new, as she's apparently been this way her entire life.

Dolores gave me my envelope with $400 and said I could leave early for my hours off in the morning. I said thank you. She was nice enough, but lo-and-behold, I have been educated here to beware of any niceties coming from either of them; it invariably reflects a storm brewing and they're just triggering my marshmallow side to put fire to it. After I rolled Roxanne back for her pee, I walked with Dolores down the hallway to the kitchen... gently told her (GENTLY, and with compassion) that I was concerned for Roxanne — that her memory is failing, as is her reality. I mentioned the meds falling into the pudding, told her about the cursive handwriting list her mother had made that night, trying to remember items she used to keep in the cupboards, and that she had said, "My memory is failing me, I feel I'm not right these days." I felt it my *duty* to tell her this.

Ahhh, cue retort. Dolores retaliated, "There's *nothing wrong* with her memory — and you're out of here tomorrow, anyway."

Is she in denial that Alzheimer's is onsetting with her mother, or is she purposefully strategizing to deposit her into the first home that becomes available with the health authority? If this *is* Alzheimer's, none of the subsidized homes will accept Roxanne. Then, of course, Dolores would find herself trapped all the more. Already, they have decided *not* to try hiring another live-in caregiver. Thankfully, it is no longer my circus or my monkeys.

I really give no serious credence to online astrology predictions, but for fun, I look at them from time to time... First, a little background. Hell House is never locked. I am told *not* to lock the doors. I do lock two of the four entry doors to the house, however. Darleen (age 72) tells me "Don't be so paranoid; we're in the middle of nowhere. There's nothing to worry about here. I don't even lock my doors at the main house."

But funny thing, however; her husband disclosed a very different reality this morning while they were visiting here at Hell House, to which the daughter snapped, "Yeah, *you* lock our doors and have locked me out a few times. I've learned to carry keys in my pocket." They *do* lock doors!

Since tonight will be my final night resident and sleeping in Hell House, ALL DOORS WILL BE LOCKED. Case closed.

SO, back to my online horoscope for today:

> "The fear of being in personal danger may force you to take some
> security precautions. Well, Sagittarius, you have every reason to
> be worried today. With the Moon and Mercury in Aquarius, you
> better be careful as the chance of an attack or break-in is relatively
> high. Keep all the doors and windows of your house closed and
> make sure they are locked at night. At this time, it is advisable not
> to let any strangers enter your house. When venturing out of the
> house, make sure you secure the premises. Astrologers advise you
> to remain extra cautious from 7:45 pm to 8:50 PM."

HOORAH! Independence day! I slept fairly well, though I woke up about six times with anxiety.

Now 7:31 AM, I have Roxanne's meds out, coffee made, porridge ready for the microwave, juices out, and her lunch made (and labeled inside the fridge)... Today is bath-girl day and I have four hours off for that timeframe.

Fire is blazing, and there is a ready supply of wood stacked inside the house that will last for a couple of days, but Dolores will need to chop more wood outside and will need kindling. I intend to use all the scrap kindling and bark I brought in today! I am not leaving any kindling possibilities for her out there, since she left *me* having to fiddle on the ground to put anything together to start a fire.

I will leave around 9:30 this morning (since Dolores said I could leave early) and will return shortly after 2 PM. I will not rush back to be on time. I truly no longer care about "going the extra mile." This is the first time in my life I have stooped to such a level.

I will give Roxanne more leftover meatloaf, the rest of the white asparagus, and some peas for dinner. I will turn her lights out (not PUNCH her lights out) at 9 PM, and I will then break down my computer, load it into the car, check on her one more time at 9:30 — and LEAVE. NEVER TO RETURN.

Dolores has not checked the mail in over a week, and I know she is purposefully failing to do that, given my departure. But, no worries, I deflected all mail a week ago, and that should circumvent anything from ever being sent here again. She considers herself smart and coy, and I look forward to leaving her to enjoy her continuing misery in my absence.

I returned to Hell House at 1:40 PM, and it was fortuitous that I arrived early. I was surprised to pull into the driveway and see no bath girl vehicle there! Dolores was putting Roxanne to bed when I walked inside. Bath girl was a no-show. Karma lurks once again!

Assessing the situation in the household, the fire was still active and Dolores had washed the dishes (I put them away). Roxanne is down for her nap and I will warm up leftovers for her at 5 PM, escort her back to bed for 8 PM, lights out at 9 PM and I am out the door, for the ultimate time, around 9:20.

Since 7:30, Roxanne has had two calls — one from Robert (her son), and now one from Eileen (her other daughter). Both of them, of course, ask if I'm gone yet (Isabel's reply is "Nope"... then I hear, "Tomorrow morning", clearly in answer to their querying when I would leave). Being the drama queen that she is, Roxanne whines to each of them, "I've been alone down here since 7:30 — Darleen came down, but she left." Yet, here I sit, eight feet away.

Ahhh, perhaps the daughter is correct — not Alzheimer's — just bitter manipulation and entitlement.

8:03 PM

Of course, not even a last trip to the bed can go smoothly with Roxanne. I suppose with me considering *my "lasts"*, she is considering *hers*, as well. This is the last chance to dig into me. Go for it.

Again, I tried being kind and civil, but we got to the commode and she played the game of trying to scoot the wheelchair closer to the commode again. I held the wheelchair solidly so she could not scoot, and being all too aware of what she was perpetrating, she turned to challenge me. I was curt, "NOPE, you need to get up STRAIGHT ahead — I don't want you pissing on me again." She said nothing and got up in the manner she has for 10 weeks *until* last night when she found this new game to play!

And Karma visits still again, too. Dolores returned to the house at 8:30. In a curt and discourteous tone, she queried "Any chance you could stay on one more week? We will, of course, pay you the $200." Such brazen idiocy; she truly must consider me a "double D" — daft and desperate.

I said, respectfully and professionally, but with no apology, "I can't. I have made other plans, but I certainly wish you all the best." With that, she stormed out with no goodbye or further adieu, and slammed the door behind her — which I promptly locked!

How we react is our Karma, how others treat us is THEIRS.

Here's to happier days ahead, and may the drama be minimized henceforth!

FEBRUARY 1, 2017

I AM OUT! Free at last! I left Hell House at 9:30 last night. And fancy this: I slept well with no sedation medication last night! Despite the apartment being less than optimal and positioned in a sketchy neighborhood, I felt so much more relaxed and safe in my own home. This would assuredly be temporary accommodation, but I had no choice but to accept the rental. Sketchy neighborhoods are still affordable, and rash rental decision-making, particularly when you are unfamiliar with the locale, seldom finds success.

Mattie phoned me at 8 AM, asking if I had made it out of the house today, did everything go okay, and added, "When do I get to see you? Can I help you get organized?"

In all conversations with Mattie in the past week at Hell House, I made sure I did not mention the conflict and disrespect in the household. It would have been far too upsetting for him, and he already had his own home conflict to endure. I kept conversational content to animal stories and videos on Facebook, and positives in his day (smoking appropriately, not stealing from any patients in the home, not seeking marijuana, and mostly staying in his room to avoid conflict). And of course, I told him my final day at "Gramma's" was smooth sailing. It's over now — the ship has sailed.

Now, I have a list of 56 projects to make the new digs a home!

Lots of firsts ahead... Just had my first coffee in my little place... Now, to begin the healing process. I hope to never find myself in a remotely similar situation in the future.

Reminder to self:
A challenge is nothing more than an opportunity to believe.

EPILOGUE

N ow, I add the women of Hell House to my memory banks and know I will face a need to redirect my thoughts away from all that transpired. Such a short timeframe, but one that felt like so much longer. I don't want to perseverate, but I don't want to lose the lesson. It's an oddity to see, with 20-20 hindsight, that when we jump off the next cliff, deal with the next TBI crisis and manage the next emergency — we gloss over the lessons that were deposited into our psyche so deeply... We send the lessons to the background — because new crisis response demands focused attention.

So often, I catch myself ruminating on something my mother said or did, or a facial response to my presence — or something an office bully, or my Ex, said to me years ago — things I thought I had forgotten until some stressor in my day brings hidden content to the surface of my mind. That's when I return to torment myself with thought — with analysis, with doubts — and when I hope to have the composure and will to redirect my thoughts away from what I know to cause self-harm.

I now label the individuals from my past, who have cemented self-doubt and emotional dysfunction within me, as "narcissists". I know that's a catch-phrase over-quoted by the masses today, but it's a phrase that most will comprehend on some level. After all, a narcissist has touched or clawed most of us in our lifetimes.

What the narcissists triggered in me over decades was lying dormant the whole time; their abuse just awakened what I needed to address to live my best life. Of course, I was too close to the forest to see the trees at the time of the abuse, but ultimately — I needed those unhappy and controlling women, my Ex, those office bullies, and those friendships who devastated me with betrayal and increased my self-doubt.

I heard someone say,

"The problem is you don't think you can do better."

Good point. In crisis with my son, in crisis with my career, in crisis with my physical and ultimately my mental health suffering, I felt I could not do better. All I could do is attempt to control how I responded to the behaviors thrust upon me — but I never stopped strategizing for a remedy, for a plan to create something better.

I needed all of those rogue villains in my life, but not in the way most think. Heck, not in the way I considered at first. In reality, I attracted them because I was a person in need — in need of help, in need of guidance, in need of empathy, and understanding. I was steering a ship with a rudder in need of repair. I attracted the reprobate that so readily found me. *That* is my ownership — and not my over-thinking the bullying imposed as something I deserved and trying to identify what I had done to deserve such harm and disrespect.

I needed the women of Hell House (and the office bullies and my mother before them) to show me how poorly I actually felt about myself, what little self-worth and respect I had to let someone treat me like they did. And hindsight being 20-20, it became easier to see why rash decision-making resulted in questionable consequences. In the same context, we can discern how a narcissist/a bully can make us question ourselves, particularly if we are an individual intent on taking ownership of "what's yours" — to create and continue self-improvement. I have always been that person. I have always held a mantra inside my mind: "Autograph your work with excellence."

More often than not, we find with 20-20 hindsight that the other side of "ownership" was never ours (e.g., what did I do to deserve this? Or, there must be a reason, and how do I take ownership of it?). The sadly twisted minds and entrapments of the narcissists brought us unnecessary doubt — but sadly, the individuals rendering the pain and resulting degradation in confidence, ability, and hope are actually suffering from the same. When the only power they could enjoy waned, they usurped the power of others when others permitted it.

A lesson learned the hard way is a lesson learned for a lifetime. And the lessons repeated for me, over time, until I accepted the gleanings from my education.

But we move forward with a plan, with hope — and with new purpose, grateful to live to fight another day, and oh so grateful to experience the love and connection between a parent and a child.

ABOUT AUTHOR

Canadian writer Sarah Martin has lived in diverse cultures such as Japan, Korea, Thailand, and Central America. No stranger to trauma and a self-described recluse now because of it, she writes from home with the inspiration of water and mountains in every view. She is known to regularly take refuge on a park bench, chatting about freedom, peace, and undying love with her son, Mattie.

ALSO BY... SARAH MARTIN

Made in the USA
Middletown, DE
30 May 2022

A Tale of Two Psyches

SARAH MARTIN

Thank you for purchasing books from my "A Tale of Two Psyches" series.

If you enjoyed reading any of the books in this series, would you consider leaving a review on Amazon.com or Amazon.ca? Amazon links each book are noted below! You can leave a review on Amazon, even if you purchased through Barnes & Noble, Apple Books or via any bookstore outlet.

	Amazon.com (USA)	Amazon.ca (Canada)
CHAOS FOR THE FLY	https://www.amazon.com/dp/1778146708	https://www.amazon.ca/dp/1778146708
HELL HOUSE	https://www.amazon.com/dp/1778200508	https://www.amazon.ca/dp/1778200508
BEFORE THE MASK SLIPS	https://www.amazon.com/dp/B0B2NQ768I	https://www.amazon.ca/dp/B0B2NQ768I
DEATH SENTENCE	*Pre-orders available, launching early July 2022*	
FREEDOM	*Launching by or before late-August 2022*	
	Launching by or before mid September 2022	

And launching by or before September 30, 2022: THE AMYGDALA RESPONSE – Dissociation as a Survival Mechanism

Thank you!